FANTASY
CARS

IAN KUAH

FANTASY
CARS

A SELECTION OF THE WORLD'S MOST DESIRABLE AUTOMOBILES
EDITED BY LAURIE CADDELL AND IAN WARD
WITH A FOREWORD BY FRANCO SBARRO

LONGMEADOW PRESS

Printed in Spain by Cayfosa,
Barcelona

ISBN 0-681-40046-3

Dep. Leg. B-25829 - 1986

Page 1
The Vestatec
Magnum, a
ferociously powerful
car lurking beneath
stylish overclothes
Previous pages
The Styling Garage
Mercedes Gullwing,
an even better
version of the classic
Mercedes sports car
This page
The electric blue
Koenig Mercedes SL
Roadster, wind-in-
the-hair motoring
with style

CONTENTS

FOREW

Being able to inspire the kind of wonder and excitement that gleams in a child's eyes at the prospect of some long-awaited treat is, for me, the essence of a life with purpose. Throughout our lives we are presented with so many inspiring subjects to enjoy and our dreams can take all sorts of different forms — self-expression through painting, the cinema or any other art form, flying or even motor cars.

As for myself, I have been gripped by a passion for cars ever since my early childhood and giving shape to my exotic creations has become my main aim in life. The realization of these dreams and the power they have to inspire fellow enthusiasts lends my handiwork an almost mystical quality.

After 35 years of hard work, I am still in business, thanks largely to those kindred spirits who have shared their dreams with me in the shape of 350 cars and 58 different models. These people have placed their trust in me, becoming

6

temporary partners. With them I need to share a certain type of upbringing and attitude, a taste for hard work and for problem-solving. It is only when a unity of purpose begins to emerge, when we have started to plan together, that putting our ideas into practice becomes possible.

In this grey, industrial, standardized world, it may seem astonishing that there is still scope for so many dreams. I believe, however, that creative outlets such as this are even more vital when we are hemmed in so tightly by the restrictions of our everyday lives.

Thanks to the car in its many guises, I am able to keep on dreaming, together with the thousands of other kindred spirits who make their presence felt by their many letters. Those who have the chance to see their ideas take shape are, of course, the privileged few. My indebtedness to them is enormous, as it is only when I come face-to-face with one of these lucky people that collaboration becomes possible.

The pages that follow contain a collection of fantastic automobiles, their spellbinding character captured in breathtaking colour photography, and I hope they will provide you with as much inspiration and enjoyment as I have found through my own contribution to the world of dream cars.

Franco Sbarro

PORSCHES 924 AND 928
ARTZ

Y ou can never have too much power,' says 44-year-old Gunter Artz, master coachbuilder and maker of some of the fastest Q-cars the motoring world has ever seen. It would seem that he practises what he preaches, both at work and in his private life.

The rest of the world saw his first creation over a decade ago in 1973, when an innocuous-looking VW Beetle began a reign of terror on the

Art for Artz' sake: the Gunter Artz Estate variation on a Porsche 924S Turbo with the bonnet and wheelarch addenda of the rare Carrera GT

Autobahns, blowing big BMWs and Mercedes into the weeds on sheer straight-line performance. What the bewildered owners of these cars did not know was that under the standard louvred engine cover of the Beetle lurked a 210bhp Porsche 911 2.7-litre Carrera power unit. It wasn't quite as simple as that, however, for a Beetle with that much power would be lethal if the engine were simply a direct replacement; in fact, the entire chassis was modified and

the Porsche unit mounted amidships to give the car handling to match its pace. Top speed was an easy 136mph (219kph).

When the Golf, VW's new bread-and-butter car, was launched in 1974, Artz was soon making plans to create the successor to his VW Carrera, but it was not until six years later, when the 300bhp Porsche 928S engine became available, that a new terror returned to the Autobahns. For drivers of the newer versions of those big BMWs and Mercedes, it was almost a case of 'just when you thought it was safe to go back in the water', and they soon found a boxy hatchback snapping at their heels which could ultimately blast past them at its 155mph (250kph) top speed and leave them floundering in its wake. To take the V8 engine and the 928S interior, the Golf was spliced down the middle and 11¾ inches (30cm) of steel added to it. There is no body-styling kit for any fancy add-ons, apart from a set of alloy wheels to take the wide P7s, so the alterations are not really immediately apparent. This very low-profile projectile became Artz's personal transport for daily use and must be the most potent 'runabout' ever!

But not all of Gunter Artz's creations are such elaborate Q-cars and he certainly could not make a living producing them. On a day-to-day basis, his firm has become famous for producing estate-car versions of popular high-performance cars which, because of their low-volume production, would never be considered by their makers. The first of these was the original VW Scirocco and a few of these conversions were sold to the Norstadt hotel chain in Hannover as stylish hold-alls. An Audi 200 Turbo Estate followed, together with a popular conversion of the Audi quattro. Fourteen of these £25,000 quattro conversions were built eventually, seven going to French buyers. His love of Porsche cars brought Artz to produce an estate version of the Porsche 924 Turbo and this was visually spruced up by using the wheel-arch extensions and bonnet air scoop from the 924 Carrera GT.

With the hot hatchback craze really warming up in 1983, Artz could not resist playing with the new Opel Corsa which, with its bulging wheel arches, looked the perfect candidate for more muscle. Looking at the Opel parts list, Artz found that the 115bhp fuel-injected engine from the Opel Kadett GTE was almost a direct swap and along with a bit of bracing to the bodyshell, particularly between the front suspension towers, Artz produced a little bombshell that left Golf GTis and Escort XR3is gasping for breath. But Artz wanted an even more powerful successor to the quattro and 924 estate. Despite its standard 928S engine, the 300bhp estate he made in 1983 has a 6mph (9.7kph) edge over the coupé, thanks to a more aerodynamic rear end. Thus, Artz holds the record for the fastest, most powerful and at £35,000, the most expensive VW Beetle ever; the fastest, most powerful and at £44,500, the most expensive VW Golf; and now, selling at £9,000 more than a stock 928S, one of the fastest estate cars in the world.

The advantages of the 928S estate do not stop at its extra load-carrying ability. The smaller rear window in a much more vertical position prevents the massive solar gain that the 928S suffers from, whilst headroom for rear passengers is vastly improved. Dog-lovers can now carry their pets in the back as well, if the animals can stand the pace, that is!

Work on this car started with the roof being removed and replaced with an entirely new section. To give this longer panel more strength, Artz incorporated a second roll-over bar into the roof at the extreme rear. Access to the deep rear compartment is aided by the tailgate hinging from a point about 1 foot (30cm) into the roof-line. This prototype tailgate was made from steel and needed its glass specially fabricated. According to Artz, it was this tailgate which gave

him a few sleepless nights and, as its weight affected the weight distribution of the car, it has now been changed for a glass fibre component. With a production run of ten units, Artz first had to sort out some of the items he was unhappy with on the prototype. These included a remote-controlled electric release for the tailgate which itself adopted less severe and more contoured lines, and the door surrounds altered to blend in with the new look of the car. A final visual touch was the 16-inch (41cm) diameter alloy wheels which were in fact experimental sets from Porsche.

Gunter Artz has built up quite a following all over Europe and has many regular customers who are always on the look-out for his latest creations. He takes commissioned work as well, so if you think you

would like the only Aston Martin Lagonda Estate in the world, Artz would be happy to oblige!

Drivers of big BMWs and Mercedes found this boxy hatchback snapping at their heels, which could blast past them and leave them floundering in its wake

Estate of the art? The Artz load-lugging variation on the Porsche 928S is a lot less bulbous than the base model. Naturally, the load area is bigger but it also solves the problem of head-room for the rear-seat passengers. The premium for this extra versatility is £9,000

ZAGATO
ASTON MARTIN

The world has witnessed the result of Aston Martin and Zagato co-operation already. In 1960, the brutishly handsome Aston Martin DB4GT Zagato successfully married Italian style and British engineering, with an elegantly curved aluminium bodyshell mounted on the Feltham-built chassis. Powerplant was an all-alloy

ARTIN

DOHC straight-six with a bank of three Weber 45 DCOE carburettors and two plugs per cylinder to give this road racer a top speed of 150mph (241kph) and 6-second 0–60mph (0–97kph) acceleration capability from 282bhp.

The announcement that history was to repeat itself with yet another liaison between the two companies was made at the 1985 Geneva

Show, where Aston Martin unveiled a scale model and artist's rendering of the new car. Unveiling of the actual cars took place at Geneva one year later in 1986, with two of the limited run of 50 cars on the Aston Martin and Zagato stands and a third on the patio of the Beau Rivage hotel overlooking the lake.

Both firms have many things in common, not the least of which is

organization size. And from the business point of view, neither had produced a new car for several years – Aston Martin since the radical Lagonda in 1978 and Zagato since designing and building specials for Alfa Romeo and Lancia in the Seventies. From that point of view, the co-operative venture gave Aston Martin the opportunity to regenerate public interest in the company and

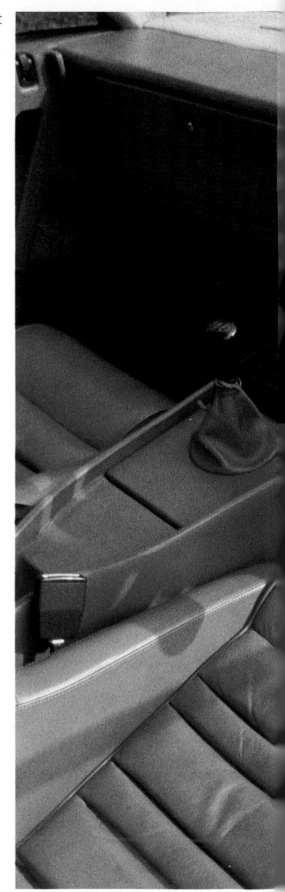

Zagato the chance to prove that it can still coachbuild cars as well as anyone else in Italy.

The finished car, like its predecessor, carries many clues as to its combined Newport Pagnell and Milanese origins. The grille shape is the distinctive Aston Martin configuration, but far more angular than ever before, while Zagato influence is clearly visible in the slightly bulged roof panel and the bonnet hump. Drag coefficient was given a lot of attention for, while the Vantage powerplant in its higher state of tune produces 435bhp at 6,200rpm and a massive 396lb ft of torque at 5,100rpm, it was Aston Martin's aim that the new Zagato should pass 180mph (290kph) easily. In the event, the quarter scale model exhibited a Cd of 0.29 in the wind tunnel and production cars with all their legally required addenda are not expected to score lower than 0.31 – a strikingly good figure when you consider that the Ferrari Testarossa, with 390bhp and clocked at 181mph (291kph), has a Cd of 0.36.

Zagato has made use of flush glass before on the recent Lancia Thema Estate prototype. On the Aston Martin Zagato, this flush glazing covers even the pillars to give a truly continuous expanse of glass. Along the flanks of the hand-beaten aluminium body, the door handles are also completely flush and the only other visible chrome plating is on the traditional grille. The blunt snout and the Kamm tail are bumpers in themselves in the contemporary fashion and are made from polyurethane-filled, glass-reinforced polyester which is resilient enough to shrug off car-park bumps,

should owners of lesser machinery let their envy get the better of them. Contoured into the nose-cone are perspex, flush-fitting light covers which protect four deeply recessed rectangular halogen units.

Giuseppe Mittino, who has been with Zagato since 1971, styled the Aston in the absence of Ercole Spada, the designer of the original 1960 car, who subsequently left the firm to work with BMW. Mittino has had to make a few changes to the original concept drawing to see the car into production and many of these have been forced upon him by pure mechanical considerations. The louvred headlamp covers, for instance, had to be deleted for the sake of lighting performance and the decision to stick with carburettors meant that the bonnet louvres have had to be replaced by a power bulge.

Wind-tunnel testing has established the need for front and rear spoilers which did not appear on the models exhibited at Geneva. Airflow beneath the car is smoothed by front and rear undertrays but at present the lift at speeds up to 150mph (241kph) is in the order of 80lb (36kg) at each end. Aston Martin would like to see downforce in the order of 120lb (54kg) at these speeds, at which point the spoilers would raise the Cd to 0.31.

Only a few changes have had to be made to the Newport Pagnell rolling chassis. The brake servos have been shifted to the rear seat area and squatter radiators and coolers are used under the lower bonnet line. Physically, the Zagato is a shorter car by all of 18 inches (46cm) and 10⅝ inches (27cm) of this is lost in the shorter rear overhang which has

Previous pages The Aston Martin Zagato flies against a tide of low, angular windcheaters with its rounded and fluid lines. Its grille is unmistakably Aston

Left and below The Zagato's looks are almost vintage, its designers continuing the Aston Martin theme of traditional materials and high-quality construction

necessitated a new boot floor panel. The 15-inch (38cm) BBS alloy wheels of the Vantage have given way to slotted 16-inch (41cm) diameter ones which carry 225/50VR16 Goodyear Eagle tyres in place of the Avons or P7s that grace the wheels of lesser Astons. A space-saver spare is used and this is identical when viewed from the side. Head-on, however, it is dramatically thinner.

The Zagato's 432bhp is some

50bhp up on the standard Vantage's output. Although the maximum torque figure is achieved at very high revs, the engine is apparently very flexible, with a second peak occurring lower down at 4,000rpm with over 350lb ft available from 3,500rpm. Gear-changing wastes time, and to improve the car's chances of breaking the 5-second mark on the 0–60mph (0–97kph) sprint, first gear will just reach that speed aided by the engine's relatively flat torque curve.

Internally, the engine uses higher-compression Cosworth pistons from 9:1 to 10.2:1 and camshafts with higher lift. The four Weber 48IDF carburettors are retained but bored out to 2 inches (50mm) and their air-

Where this car scores is in exclusivity. Zagato will only ever make 50 of these cars and for collectors, this makes the £87,000 price tag a bargain

box casing has been redesigned with a lower profile to clear the new bonnet line. Even so, the hump in the bonnet is the result of their intrusion. While on cars of this price and exclusivity it is normal to make engineering changes as a concession to styling, in the case of the Vantage engine, fuel injection which could have achieved the desired lower engine profile was considered but then rejected as it would have taken too long to develop. A special big bore exhaust system also helps the power.

While the new car's cockpit contains improvements such as a more effective ram-fed heater duct system at the base of the windscreen, a tilting steering wheel and better-laid-out instruments, the loss of space imposed by the shorter wheelbase must be lamented. The rear seat has been edged out to be replaced with a small bench suitable only for luggage. Of course, if you regard the car as a large two-seater, the bench may be welcomed, as luggage room in the boot has also been diminished!

The instrument pack is Vantage in origin but is now more upright in layout and directly in front of the driver rather than being spread out. The use of materials like leather and wood remains, in traditional Aston Martin style, but the excellent fixed backrest seats which bear more than a passing resemblance to those in the Lancia Delta S4 homologation special, are clearly Zagato.

The objective for the new car was

simple: 186.4mph (300kph) and 0–60mph (0–97kph) in under 5 seconds. The £87,000 price tag puts the Zagato firmly in the league of other specials like the Ferrari GTO at £73,000 and the Porsche 959 at £110,000 but, while the Italian and German rivals use a lot of very modern, high-tech engineering such as twin-turbocharging and, in the case of the Weissach machine, four-wheel-drive, the Aston relies on traditional cubic inches and on a well developed, front-engined, rear-driven design. It can match its rivals on straight roads, although perhaps not round corners, but where the Zagato scores is in exclusivity. While Porsche has been persuaded to make 250 rather than 200 959s, Zagato will only ever make 50 cars for Aston Martin. For collectors, this must make the £87,000 outlay seem a bargain.

Left Compared to a Testarossa or a Countach, the Zagato looks a little dated. Underneath the surprisingly aerodynamic body, however, beats the powerful A-M V8

Far left Zagato has retained a particular style over the past 20 years, with high rears and bulbous flanks. This Aston differs markedly from the angles of the William Towns original

b + b

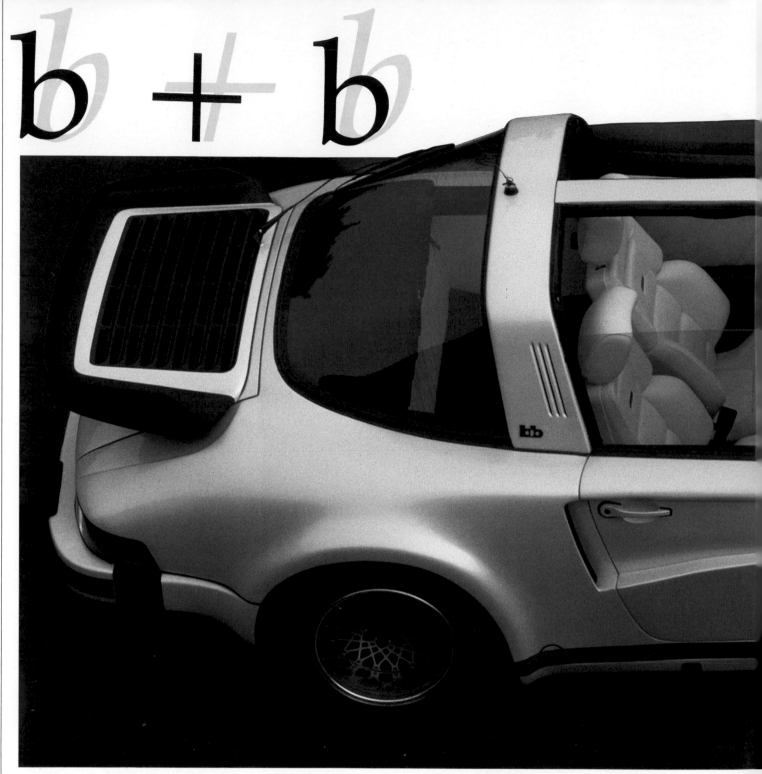

PORSCHE 911 TURBO TARGA

b + b

There is a school of thought which maintains that nothing is more crisis-proof than exclusivity. In times of economic adversity, the truly wealthy always seem able to continue to afford the best things in life and, if one makes a living catering purely for the needs of the rich, then a steady income is more or less assured, no matter what the economic climate.

This way of thinking has steered Rainer Buchmann's business

successfully through two oil crises and he is now one of the automobile industry's most respected figures. It all started when Buchmann, born in 1945, was a student of economics and engineering and managed to buy himself a Porsche from the money he earned repairing those cars in his spare time.

It was late in 1973, when the first oil crisis had bitten deep and the citizens of central Europe were having to adjust to speed limits and car-less Sundays for the first time ever,

This car was designed deliberately to fill a gap in the Porsche range. In the 911 Turbo Targa, b + b provided an open version of what Porsche aficionados revere as their most sacred icon

that Buchmann began seriously to launch his career in the motor industry. He set up his company, b + b, in a small rented workshop in his home town of Frankfurt with the aim of upgrading Porsches. Everyone thought he was mad to do this at a

Although b + b pioneered the variations on a Porsche 911 theme, its cars now look restrained. It was the first to use the 935-like snout with 928 headlamps

time when the motor car had come to be regarded as rather a liability, but Buchmann was astute enough to realize the resilience of the luxury end of the market.

If the oil crisis was central to the timing of the company's launch, then the reasoning behind it was that major manufacturers do not have the flexibility or capacity for development to take into account the needs of individual customers. That leaves the field clear for independent companies such as b + b, and the second half of the Seventies saw Buchmann go from strength to strength as he established a reputation for himself.

After three years spent upgrading the paintwork and interior trim of his clients' Porsches, Buchmann made his first international mark in 1976. A Porsche 911 to which he had applied a striking paint finish became the focus of attention at 'Photokina', the biennial international photo salon in Cologne. The car was designed deliberately to fill a gap in the Porsche range, for the factory did not have a 911 Turbo Targa, and b + b provided an open version of what Porsche aficionados revere as their most sacred icon. It was this breathtaking £29,600 car which aroused more than a little interest in magazines ranging from *Auto Motor und Sport* to *Playboy* and even further afield in the prestigious Japanese quarterly *Car Styling*, which is aimed specifically at the car-designing fraternity.

The b + b company made full use of the Dinfos on-board computer, which looks after most functions of the car. The owner could be excused for demanding that a co-driver (or even DJ!) is always on hand to take care of the dashboard full of controls

It is obviously feasible to turn the 911SC or Carrera into a convertible by removing the roof and strengthening the floorpan and sills – as Porsche itself has been doing since 1983. The completely different roof structure and integral roll-over bar of the Targa meant, however, that is was easier to put the Turbo engine and suspension into that car and modify the bodywork rather than to try and make the car from a 911 Turbo. This logical step was taken, but in true b + b fashion the final result had to have a more distinct identity. Hence the adoption of the flat nose with its large under-bumper air intake; the sculptured intakes on subsequent production cars leading into the flared bodywork at the rear which provide extra engine and brake cooling; and of course the directionally slotted b + b alloy wheels designed by former Porsche employee Eberhard Schulz. Structurally, the solution that Buchmann's designers later adopted to overcome the flexing problems generated by the tremendous torque of the 300bhp turbo engine was to turn the car into a 'T-top' by adding a horizontal member between the top of the front windscreen and the roll-over bar. The single-piece Porsche Targa roof was then replaced by two separate and individually detachable panels like those on the then current Datsun 280ZX and several American

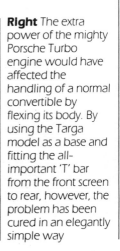**Right** The extra power of the mighty Porsche Turbo engine would have affected the handling of a normal convertible by flexing its body. By using the Targa model as a base and fitting the all-important 'T' bar from the front screen to rear, however, the problem has been cured in an elegantly simple way

cars. This solution has carried through to other b + b targa conversions, notably the Porsche 928S (see pages 26-33).

The original black Turbo Targa show car could well have labelled b + b as purely a modifier of Porsche cars but a happy coincidence had brought Buchmann and Eberhard Schulz together. Schulz brought with him tremendous experience and just as important, the complete plans and half-built prototype for the CW311, his personal interpretation of a Mercedes 300SL for the Eighties (see pages 86-97).

As a result, observers who had been prepared to write off b + b as a firm which might be very good at retrimming and repainting Porsches but which had no history of conceiving and building cars of its own, were made to sit up and take notice of this exciting partnership. In the next few years the world was to see the tangible proof of its talents.

A quick glance is hardly enough to distinguish the b + b Targa Turbo from lesser standard models, but there has been much modification. Witness the rear-flank air scoops which start from the leading edge of the doors. The directional wheels, with unsubtle arrowing, have slots which extract hot air from the hard-worked disc brakes within

b + b

PORSCHE 928S
TARGA AND CABRIOLET

b + b

Having made a name for himself with his Porsche 911 Turbo Targa (see pages 18-25) and a luxury Mercedes conversion which was the forerunner of a whole range of stylized coupés, Buchmann was adamant that he would not continue to make his living from a borrowed 'image'. He wanted something uniquely his that would attract as much attention. The age of the electronic car had just begun and there was a certain magic to the word 'digital' which seemed to excite interest wherever it appeared, and so b + b hit upon replacing conventional analogue instrumentation with a digital information system as its next project.

Once more, the right man put in an appearance at the right time. Physicist Peter Roggendorf joined the team to evolve 'Dinfos', the world's first functioning electronic dashboard, which made its debut at the 1979 Frankfurt IAA.

Dinfos, which is the acronym for Digital Information System, used large LED digits to show speed and engine rpm and triggered off the discussions that are still raging today about the relative merits of analogue and digital. But behind that seemingly simple panel lay a microcomputer which could turn its hand to calculating, storing and selectively supplying information such as average speed, fuel consumption and mileage, even if

the battery were to be disconnected or fail.

Buchmann was determined that Dinfos should be for the masses and not just another plaything for the rich. As a start he decided to install Dinfos in a demonstration fleet of ten VW Golf GTi Cabriolets, all of which bore body-styling kits and alloy wheels and were each finished in a spectacular paintwork scheme of the kind for which b + b had become famous.

To consolidate his reputation Buchmann was seeking the direct interest of and involvement with a major manufacturer. And this was soon forthcoming when Munich-based BMW announced that it was looking for a study for the motor

The chopped Targa 928 Porsche is less attractive than the smoothly proportioned original, but it allows for fresh-air motoring rather than the conditioned-air climate of Porsche's original. The heavy nose design goes some way to redressing the balance of the look, however. Note the front window quarter-lights which are absent on a 928 Coupé

For the Porsche-lover who
wants an open version of his
favourite model, the trip to the
b + b offices is the start of a
dream come true

cycle of the future. A study was
commissioned from b + b and this
became the BMW Futuro which
bristled with every conceivable item
of trim and electronic gadgetry. For
the first time, the company's
resources were stretched to the limit
and b + b fought hard to meet the
tight scheduling which is always a
result of working with a member of
the motor manufacturing
establishment. After many sleepless
nights, the finished prototype was
wheeled into the International
Bicycle and Motor Cycle Exhibition in
September 1980 bang on time.

It had taken Buchmann nearly
eight years to attain these goals, but
this was just the beginning. Now
that he had been accepted by the
industry, work was beginning to
flood in and b + b found itself in
partnership with Volkswagen, which
wanted the Dinfos system fitted to a
limited run of the new VW Polo for
research purposes.

In the early days, the dramatic and
beautifully finished b + b products
used to emerge from rather seedy
premises in the Frankfurt suburb of
Bornheim. As his success grew,
Buchmann realized that he must
acquire a suitable image for his
company in keeping with its
commercial achievements. To this
end, b + b moved to eastern
Frankfurt to a site ten times as large
which has an almost American-style
grandeur. Overseas expansion has
also come about, and a US office has
been set up in California to tap the

The interior of the
b + b Convertible
928 is little changed
except for the *de
rigueur* radio
telephone and a
mini stereo rack
system inserted into
the car's swooping
centre console. Fully
power-adjustable
Recaro seats are
incorporated, with
bright rainbow
striping to break up
the otherwise
sombre interior

Main picture The deeper spoiler of the b + b car has a more purposeful air than the original and hints at race-track compatibility. The 928 has been criticized for being bland; the b + b conversion boldly answers that

Insets Letting form get in the way of function: there can be few more inaccessible places for controls than above the driver's head, where the Clarion installation on the Targa 928 is found

lucrative American market.

Whilst b + b has diversified its interests considerably within the wide sphere of the motor industry, its work on Mercedes, Porsche and Volkswagen cars has in no way diminished. In 1984 b + b showed both a Mercedes 500SEC convertible with a power-operated roof panel that slid back, and a body-styling package for the latest Golf.

The new generation of front-engined water-cooled Porsches has not escaped Buchmann's attention either. In 1979, when the 928 was still a relative newcomer, Buchmann's team was quick off the mark with a targa-topped version. For this conversion, the entire silhouette of the car was altered and instead of a fastback coupé, the b + b creation became a notchback-booted car in profile. Structural integrity was preserved by strengthening the boot and roll-over-bar areas and once again the 'T-top' configuration was used for resistance to flexing. Early Porsche 928s were very 'clean' in profile, without the front and rear spoilers of the 928S cars. They suffered somewhat from sensitivity to crosswinds at high speeds and to counter this problem, Buchmann had his designers redraw the nose cone of the car to incorporate a substantial chin spoiler in its moulding. The possible dual use of the T-bar in the roof was explored and the team at b + b hit upon the rather bizarre idea of installing the Clarion component stereo equipment in the driver's side of that bar. While it may have been a novel idea, and perhaps Buchmann's interpretation of the concept of an internal roof console to house stereo gear, the implications of adjusting the system while on the move do not bear thinking about.

When the factory 928S arrived, complete with spoilers, Buchmann had already conceptualized a true open, two-seater version with far more elegant proportions than the somewhat ungainly Targa – the Cabriolet. The fabric hood on this car folds back neatly and is covered by a flap in the same colour as the body.

A basic 928S costs £29,600 in Germany and the conversion adds a further £25,000 to this. If you are planning some cold-weather motoring, you may wish to invest another £3,000 in a hard top for your Cabriolet.

Over 70 b + b variations on the Porsche theme leave Frankfurt every year for destinations around the world. Porsche still has no answer to the b + b 911 Turbo Targa, so for the Porsche-lover who wants an open version of his favourite model, the trip to the b + b offices is the start of a dream come true.

Pure elegance: much more aesthetically pleasing is the full open-top conversion on the Porsche 928S. Gone is the rear Targa screen, with just the smooth waistline of the standard car left to dominate this classic

LAMBORGHINI ATHON

BERTONE

Incredible though it may seem, two decades have elapsed since the very first Lamborghini prototype howled through the factory gates. And twenty years is a long time to have been building uncompromising and very fast motor cars, fraught as this business is with commercial pitfalls and a barrage of environmental constraints.

Bertone never lacks originality. Who else could give a mid-engined Lamborghini a truck-like rear and still allow it to ooze aggressive style?

Perhaps we have Enzo Ferrari to thank for the great works to come from the Lamborghini stable. In the mid-Sixties, Ferrari turned down a request from tractor manufacturer and industrialist, Ferruccio Lamborghini, to build a very special sports car. Lamborghini decided to build the car for himself and chose the symbol of a raging bull to challenge the Ferrari prancing horse.

This car was the 350GT.

It was followed by the Jarama, Espada, Muira, the dramatic Countach and the Urraco, the Bertone-designed dream machines of the late Sixties and early Seventies. Today, it is only the Countach and the Jalpa who can trace their roots back to the Urraco. Both are uncompromising, two-seater sports cars which sell surprisingly well.

The Athon is an uncompromising marriage of state-of-the-art technology and styling — an expression of confidence in the very future of car design

It was the Urraco that was the undoing of Lamborghini. A brilliant concept evolved from the design strengths of cars that Ferruccio admired, the essence of the idea came from the Porsche 911, the suspension from the Lotus 12 and the engine placement from Lamborghini's own Muira. But it took too long to get under way, and too much time and money were spent on sorting out a factory. The prototype was unveiled at the 1970 Turin Show but strikes and other delays kept the car from the hands of its first owners until May 1973. By that time, new challengers had emerged and of course there was the first oil crisis to contend with. In June 1981 the wealthy Mimram family stepped in to pull the company back from the brink of disaster.

The Athon, the Bertone styling exercise shown at the 1980 Turin Motor Show, was based on the Lamborghini Urraco for two reasons. The chassis of the Urraco was outstandingly good amongst cars of its kind and the quad-cam, 3.0-litre, 252bhp engine was powerful and responsive enough to give the Athon the performance to match its looks. Secondly, Bertone, who had worked well with Lamborghini, wanted to help the ailing firm.

The car is a Bertone classic, an aggressive sporting prototype whose design has been executed with a refreshing freedom. With the driver exposed to the elements, it is an attempt to capture the exhilaration of a Grand Prix racing car in a road car. Even standing still, the car has the dynamism of movement at speed. There has been no attempt at weather protection; this is purely and simply a fair-weather machine.

The driver sits in the middle of the car, so low that only his head is visible from outside. The only piece of glass in the car, the front windscreen, curves tightly around the cockpit into the doors. The massive engine cover is reminiscent of that of a speedboat and ends in a neatly integrated spoiler with some very elegant detailing. The rocker panel along the side of the car is, in the contemporary imagery of aerodynamics, intended to mirror the ground-effect skirts on a racing car. These 'running boards' turn up at their ends to form the leading edges of the rear wheel arches, and with another neat detail provide a natural location for the engine air-intake slots.

The shut lines and shapes Bertone has used on the Athon are innovative and exciting and relate to the speed and power housed within its sleek silhouette. The Athon is an image-conscious car, unmistakably Bertone in origin. This is what Bertone himself has to say about it: 'The choice of theme was made to stress a formula that represents to car connoisseurs total contact with nature. For people who have locked themselves in comfortable and silent shells, driving a roadster is an exciting experience.'

With a philosophy like this, it is clear that inspired designers like Bertone are far from being trapped by the efficient packaging doctrine that has pervaded the world of the utilitarian production car in recent years.

Inset, far left The driver sits close to the Athon's nose *(à la Formula One car)*, in front of digital instrumentation
Inset, left More importantly, there lurks behind the push of a four-cam V8 Lamborghini, with power for 150mph (242kph) and a wail to awaken the dead

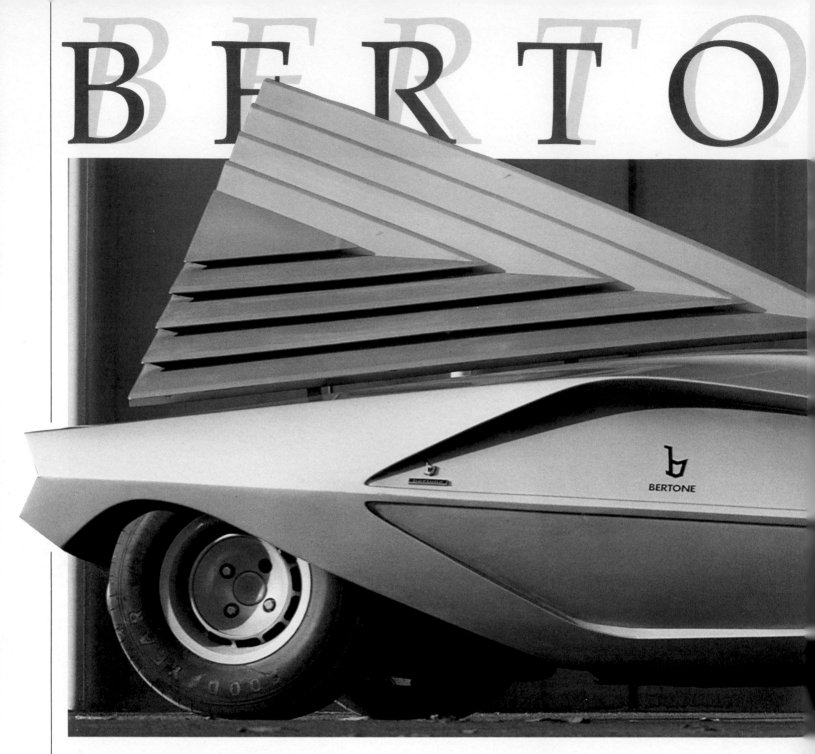

LANCIA STRATOS
BERTONE

In 1985 Lancia had an excellent World Rally Championship, with its Delta S4 chalking up an impressive Lombard RAC Rally win on its first outing. This convincing victory had been well orchestrated by the car's designers, and the unique application of supercharging as well as turbocharging to the 2-litre, twin-cam engine demonstrated that the Italians hadn't missed a trick in compensating for the turbo lag that plagues competitors like the Audi quattro and Peugeot 205 T16.

Such technical innovation is not unusual at Lancia and indeed it was over-complexity, together with somewhat old-fashioned features and high prices which made Lancias progressively more difficult to sell towards the close of the Sixties. The proud company, founded by Vincenzo Lancia, a brilliant racing driver in his youth, slowly began to bow under the weight of its mounting debts.

The climate of the Italian motor industry at this time was uneasy, as many small yet well-known companies were taken over by the huge and powerful Fiat empire steered by Agnelli. Fiat dominated the Italian industry; indeed it is sometimes said that Fiat *is* Italy. Typical of state-owned companies, Alfa Romeo lacked commercial aggression, so this left the field clear for Fiat to manipulate the rest of the industry.

The first development which eventually led to the birth of the Lancia Stratos was Fiat's underpinning of Ferrari. In June 1969, it acquired a 50 per cent shareholding in Ferrari and wisely left Enzo and his team free to continue to develop in the way they knew best. The situation at Lancia was more serious, however, and the company that traded under the shield and flag emblem was losing money quickly. When the marque of Lancia came under the wing of the Fiat empire in 1969, Fiat paid the nominal sum of one lira per share; the grand total of all the Lancia shares involved in this deal amounted to the staggering sum of £670! But Fiat also agreed to guarantee all of Lancia's debts, which amounted to the rather more substantial figure of £67,000,000. With a large injection of capital to revitalize the company, Fiat set about the development of a new line of cars to replace the ageing Fulvia and Flavia ranges. This was to emerge as the Fiat twin-cam-powered Beta range.

In the meantime, Bertone had chosen Lancia Fulvia 1600HF mechanicals as the basis for his 1970 Turin Show car. Bertone had established something of a theme in the late Sixties with dramatic wedge-shaped show cars that looked to the natural world for inspiration. The Carabo, for example, which made its

debut at Paris in 1968, was reminiscent of the carabo beetle, both in form and in its green and black colouring. This car was chosen to represent the motor car in the Museum of Twentieth Century Art in Vienna four years later. The Lamborghini Urraco continued Bertone's theme in 1970, but the

Lancia Stratos was the most outrageous of the trio.

The name 'Stratos' was thought up by Bertone and seems a logical choice for this unworldly-looking vehicle that could easily have come from beyond the stratosphere. The car was to fulfil two roles

Previous pages The dart-like profile of the Stratos, with its over-stylized engine cover opened. As a styling exercise it stopped shows, but as a practical form of transport it would have been a nightmare with its lack of visibility. The side windows would help little in guiding the car

Right The Stratos looks sleeker than a fighter aircraft, its line spoiled only by a periscope-like rear-view mirror hung in the airstream. It looks like a refugee from a futuristic film

The dart-shaped profile of the Stratos becomes even more dramatic when the triangulated engine cover is raised; entering the car is a new experience, even for those weaned on gullwing doors!

simultaneously: the design itself was for a dream car that would see the light of day at the 1970 Turin Show, whilst it was also intended to be Lancia's successor to the Fulvia HF Coupé which was being outclassed seriously in rallying by the Alpine-Renault A110 and Porsche 911.

By luck or by foresight a common factor of these two seemingly unrelated roles was the suitability of

Right and below
The front glazed panel of the Stratos hinges upwards from the front, leaving just a small nose to step over to enter the cockpit. You then lower yourself into the seats ahead of the blind rear bulkhead and complete the cocoon by lowering the 'door'. Practicality never interferes with cars built as art forms

BERTONE

Above and left
Ironically, beneath the gargantuan, wing-like engine cover lurks one of the most compact power units available, the two-cam V4 engine as used in the Lancia Fulvia HF. The engine, mated to a five-speed gearbox, drives the production car's front wheels, but turns the rears in this classic mid-engined design study

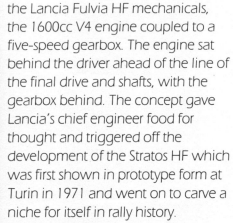

the Lancia Fulvia HF mechanicals, the 1600cc V4 engine coupled to a five-speed gearbox. The engine sat behind the driver ahead of the line of the final drive and shafts, with the gearbox behind. The concept gave Lancia's chief engineer food for thought and triggered off the development of the Stratos HF which was first shown in prototype form at Turin in 1971 and went on to carve a niche for itself in rally history.

The dart-shaped profile of the Stratos is broken only by the window panels on each side of the cockpit, set into a symmetrical indentation in the sides. The visual integrity of the whole is maintained by a line that starts from the nose, traces the top of the front wheel arch, accentuates the two halves of the side panels and then vanishes with the tail of the car. It is beautifully and simply done. The top of the side indentation is cleverly used as an engine air intake and its distance from the rest of the bodywork gives strong shadow relief to the flat surfaces of the car's sides. The simple side profile becomes even more dramatic when the unusual triangulated engine cover is raised on its side hinges.

Entering the Stratos is a new experience, even for those weaned on cars with gullwing doors! The flat, glazed canopy is rear-hinged and swings up to allow you to drop yourself in, having pivoted on the top of the wheel arch. To close the canopy, you pull it down with the steering wheel and column.

While dream cars cost a lot of money to develop and make, Nuccio Bertone maintains that they have practical applications, too: 'When a client asks for some innovative solution in record time, we generally have one already available in one of our show cars'. Nevertheless, the pleasure for Bertone obviously lies in producing cars that are real show-stoppers and can cause ripples of sensation at international shows and keep his staff in high spirits.

When the Bertone Stratos appeared as a 'production' car, it differed in almost every respect to its namesake. Gone was the Lancia V4 engine, replaced by a Ferrari Dino V6 power unit, which gave this purpose-built rally car shattering performance. Nothing as specialized as the Stratos had been seen before on the rally stages of the world, and those that shared events with it usually only saw its rear as it raced off into the distance to reach the chequered flag first. It was good to see designer clothing used on such a functional chassis!

MERCEDES 190E 5.0 AND 500SEC/SEL
BRABUS

Rich or not so rich, there will always be those who prefer to travel without attracting attention but are not willing to give up performance or luxury. For wealthy customers of Brabus Autosport, tuning wing of the largest Mercedes-Benz dealer in north-west Germany, the solution is to shoehorn a tuned version of the largest production Mercedes engine into the engine bay of the smallest Mercedes car, the 190. The result of this power transplant is a 250bhp 5.0-litre V8-powered 190E that does 160mph (257kph) flat-out and accelerates from 0–60mph (0–97kph) in a shattering 4.8 seconds, a performance that the latest Porsche 911 Carrera cannot better.

To cope with twice the rated horsepower of a standard 190E and the extra weight up front, the Brabus car has had to be almost completely

re-engineered in the chassis. Shorter, uprated springs are fitted along with special dampers from Sachs, a modified rear axle from the 500SE with limited-slip differential and a specially made propeller shaft to take the massive torque transmitted through the four-speed manual gearbox. Should you feel that the Getrag four-speed is not giving the best possible acceleration, then you can order a close-ratio ZF five-speed box or if your pace through life is more leisurely, then Brabus will save itself the effort of unbolting the four-speed automatic box from the 500SE engine. Fortunately, the four contact patches of rubber glueing this very powerful car to the road are suitably large Pirelli P7 tyres of 225/50VR15 size on 7 × 15-inch (18 × 38cm) Rial alloy wheels which contribute to the car's stability under full throttle – at least in the dry.

Subtlety is the hallmark of Brabus conversions, with just the attractive wheels and minor styling changes to give the game away. Underneath the 500SEC (above) and the 190E (left), there is a wealth of change, from heavily uprated chassis to splendidly modified engines

Going fast is one thing, stopping quite another. The 190E 5.0 thus carries larger-diameter, slotted and vented disc brakes at the front and larger solid discs at the rear.

As with all Brabus-converted cars, the visual additions to the bodywork consist of a front spoiler, side skirts and a rear undertray. All of these have concealed fittings so there are no exposed screw heads to spoil the illusion of the neatly integrated styling kit, which is aesthetically low-key but aggressive enough to give the car authority in the overtaking lane. Unlike most of its competitors, Brabus does not sanction the use of bolt-on boot-lid spoilers, saying that these do not suit the up-market image of Mercedes-Benz products. Instead, they blend a subtle raised lip into the trailing edge of the boot lid using glass fibre and a lot of craftsman's skill.

A fact that will console that wealthy owner travelling incognito is that while he may have sacrificed space inside and the amount of sheet metal around him, no concession has had to be made in quality, for all Mercedes-Benz cars are made to a consistent standard, whether they be the little 190E or the big 500SEL. In line with the manufacturer's philosophy, Brabus can also install in the 'mini-major' Mercedes, most of the trim and gadgetry that are listed as options only on the larger cars.

Thus a 190E 5.0-owner can have the benefit of wood cappings on the doors to match the dashboard and centre console; electrically operated Recaro seats trimmed in cloth or leather from a wide selection of colours, textures and grades; and any in-car entertainment that he fancies, from a simple Panasonic radio/cassette to a 300-watt Nakamichi system with sub-woofers. Whatever, part of the basic package and an invaluable aid to keeping a grip on things, is the special leather-covered Brabus four-spoke steering wheel which comes in three different rim thicknesses to suit driver preference. Also mandatory is a 190mph (300kph) speedometer and matching

BRABUS

rev counter incorporating an oil temperature gauge. But beware of the options list, for while the £32,000 asking price of the car illustrated here includes engine, suspension, wheels and tyres, body kit and the Recaro seats, Brabus customers have been known to spend as much as £11,000 on an antique-leather-trimmed interior and sub-woofered, bi-amped sound system alone and that amounts to the price of a new Mercedes 190E!

Brabus, the acronym of Brackmann and Buschmann, was started in the mid-Seventies by those two entrepreneurs. Today the staff count is 45, a third of the workers of the parent company, Auto Buschmann. With a father in the car business for over 30 years, Bodo Buschmann, who heads Brabus Autosport, grew up with the proverbial steering

wheel in his hands. In the early Seventies, he had a Mercedes 250 with lowered suspension and wider tyres on alloy wheels, on which he persuaded his workshop staff to perform some tweaks and find another 20bhp through fairly simple engine modifications. This sparked off a run on the place because suddenly, customers wanted similar alterations and Buschmann had to start up a separate operation to cater for this specialized work.

At one point, Brabus Autosport

Underneath the minor changes to the Mercedes-Benz 500SEC body (left) lurks a 5-litre engine (above) whose output is boosted by a Paxton supercharger. The unit, which is driven directly from the crankshaft, boosts the power output of the standard car to well over 300bhp, pushing the coupé into the supercar performance league

was also the largest AMG dealer in its region but a conflict of opinions forced a parting of the ways. The buying climate in Germany at the time was very conducive to the development of the vast tuning industry that now exists, and as it was obviously too profitable and interesting a business to let go, Auto Buschmann decided to market a spoiler, tuning and suspension programme under the Brabus name.

Another reason for having its own product line was the feeling that what was available on the market for Mercedes-Benz was not in keeping with the image or character of the cars. In particular, it was felt that the modified suspensions were too firm for the average Mercedes owner and the aerodynamic additions looked tagged-on and heavy. Thus Brabus set out to design its parts in such a way that a Brabus Mercedes is still a Mercedes, with spoilers and side skirts that accentuate and integrate rather than conflict with the original lines of the cars.

As far as interiors are concerned, plastic is not quite the thing, and only traditional quality materials like leather and wood are used. Many grades of leather are stocked and the customer can spend anything between £5,500 and £9,000 for a re-trim, depending on the quality of the leather. Currently, the favoured choice is antique leather, which has marble-like colour patterns in it. A car takes four to six weeks to re-trim completely, and the work can be done at the same time as the engine and body alterations. The company

The Brabus 190E is a Q-car *par excellence*. In place of the standard car's 2-litre, four-cylinder engine there is a 5-litre V8 from its larger 500-range stablemate

has so far produced a small run of four 190E 5.0 cars with differing standards of options for its customers, and the original car remains at Brabus Autosport as a dramatically fast engineering showpiece.

As the ultimate Q-car, the little 5-litre 190 scores full marks. But for the wealthy who believe that if you've got it you should flaunt it, and who prefer to start off with the big

A very complete example of a full-house 500SEL costs a mighty £56,000 — cheaper than the closely-matched Bentley Mulsanne Turbo, in case you're watching the pennies!

500SEC or SEL, the 5-litre engine in these machines can be given a boost with a supercharger. The American-made Paxton unit adds 90bhp to the

Far left The big Mercedes V8 engine is a more-than-snug fit in the 190E's engine bay, but the conversion is excellently finished. The motor endows the Mercedes baby with a verve which is lacking in the original

Left The cramped cockpit of the 190E has been suitably spiced with Recaro seats, a grippy wheel and a stereo system which would fill a large concert hall with its decibels

existing 231bhp and will advance the 1.5-ton projectile close to the 160mph (257kph) mark.

This £4,300 addition works all the way through the engine speed range to expand the entire performance envelope. To put things in perspective, the 0–125mph (0–201kph) time of the blown Brabus 500SEC is 26 seconds, against 41 seconds for the standard car. Lower and stiffer suspension, once again using Sachs components, is added and huge Pirelli P7s of 225/50VR16 on 8 inch (20cm) wide Rial alloys fill out the arches in front, with even bigger 245/45VR16s on 9 inch (23cm) wide wheels at the rear.

A subtle body kit is added which enhances the slight wedge-shape of the Mercedes bodywork and once again a bespoke interior can be fitted. A very complete example of such a car would cost a mighty £56,000, still cheaper than a Bentley Mulsanne Turbo, though, which in purpose if not actual effect, must be the car most closely matched on paper to a full-house 500SEL.

BUICK

WILDCAT
BUICK

Despite the Buick Wildcat's amazing futuristic appearance, its origins in fact stem from 1953 when its forebear fulfilled much the same role as a show car and experimental test-bed. Those were early days for the glass fibre material so widely used today and the bodyshell of the first Wildcat was a first move to study the feasibility of using GRP in production. Two more Wildcat concept cars were unleashed on the world before 1962, when Buick deemed the name meant enough to the public to be carried over to a production car. With reversion of the Wildcat designation to a concept car in 1985, the story of

this streamlined supercar has come full circle.

In commissioning the project, the management of Buick specified that it was not in search of a 'single mission' vehicle aimed solely at the attainment of speed, aerodynamics or avant-garde styling, but rather an amalgamation of all these virtues and more. The final package is thus a harmonious integration of design, structure, powerplant, electronics and accommodation – a concept with practicality.

The Wildcat has been described as a unique blend of art and engineering, of flowing sculptured surfaces punctuated by exposed mechanical elements. Buick has a

strong reputation, built up on road and racing cars, for technical innovation in V6 configuration engines, and part of the initial brief for the Wildcat was to emphasize this with an aesthetically pleasing power unit of functional beauty and high casting quality. Thus, the mid-mounted 231-cubic inch (3.8-litre) engine goes for power efficiency and looks, with the logical extension of four valves per cylinder and twin-overhead camshafts per cylinder bank to achieve an output of 230bhp at 6,000rpm and 245 lb ft of torque at 4,000rpm.

A high-output, sequential, electronic Cross-Fire Fuel-Injection System was specially developed for

the engine, and this features precalibrated fuel delivery according to a computer 'map' based on throttle position, manifold depression, ambient temperature and engine rpm. This electronic SFI system, a development of a current production unit, is field-programmable to allow precise adjustment of the fuel flow rate from inside the vehicle.

With such high power and torque figures available, both front- or rear-wheel-drive begin to look inadequate for all-weather transfer of output into traction. Buick engineers thus opted for permanent four-wheel-drive with a transfer casing attached to the rear of the gearbox

Right The interior of the Buick Wildcat has two separate sculptured positions for driver and passenger

Above As many functions as possible are crammed into the steering-wheel area. Such features appeal more to the designer than they do to the driver, however. The central display indicates horsepower produced and *g* force generated, the sort of information which is useful after rather than during the event of driving

housing, transferring power via a chain drive to the torque splitter which apportions the power 34/66 per cent front to rear, a ratio which balances the torque output to the vehicle's weight distribution. The transmission itself is a modified form of an existing General Motors (GM) four-speed automatic.

The Wildcat is independently suspended by adjustable coil-over-shock absorbers and unequal-length wishbones at each corner, with fine tuning by an anti-roll bar at each end. The 8 × 16-inch (20 × 41cm) and 9 × 16-inch (23 × 41cm) alloy wheels carry 225/50VR16 tyres all round. In line with current thinking on active primary safety, the car is equipped with computer-controlled ABS anti-lock braking.

Despite the predominance of heavy mechanical components, weight is kept to 2,910lb (1,310kg) by use of the latest composite materials such as carbon fibre. The body is made from this material as well as GRP and vinyl-ester, while the floorpan is an 1/8 inch (3mm)-thick laminate of the three.

At the front, a steel sub-frame carries the suspension, power-

***The Wildcat is a harmonious
integration of design, structure,
powerplant, electronics and
accommodation — a combination
rarely seen in competitive
production cars***

steering, brake master cylinder and
axle housing while the rear sub-
frame mounts the engine,
suspension, twin-radiators and foam-
filled 15-gallon (68-litre) fuel-cell. No
chassis structure as such is used, the
sub-frames being directly attached to
the laminate structure.

The dramatic styling of the Wildcat
was developed under the supervision
of Charles M. Jordan, Director of
Design at GM, and the job was
initially handed to Buick Design
Studio No. 1. Such a deviation from
the norm was desired, however, that
the task had to be farmed out to
several sources. Buick Design Studio
No. 2 and students from the
automobile design class at the Center
for Creative Studies in Detroit tackled
the assignment, but it was not until
the summer of 1984 that the correct
theme was hit upon. It was David P.
Rand, a senior designer in Studio No.
1, who created the shape that drew

all the elements together. A radical departure from the traditional GM profile of long bonnet and short boot, the mid-engined arrangement is unusual in that it has a long rear deck which is ideal for highlighting the exposed engine. Rand's drawings were converted to a scale model and shifted to GM's Advanced Design Studio No. 2, where several major contributions were made to the final exterior design. The head-on silhouette is unbroken in line, with no interruptions for cabin or glass. The form of the transparent canopy integrates into the front wings while the rear of the canopy flows into the engine deck.

Access to the passenger compartment is via a raised canopy made from cast grey acrylic and carbon fibre with glass-reinforced polyester resin. In keeping with the car's space-age image, this canopy is raised as a single unit once its exterior latches have been unlocked by a solenoid. For ease of entry, the steering wheel tilts upwards with the canopy and the occupants then sit on the low, wide sills and swing their legs into the compartment.

To ensure a unified theme, the sculptured interior was designed in conjunction with the exterior. The driver's seat is power-adjustable in eight different ways, including inflatable lumbar and side supports.

Primary instrumentation is displayed in the centre of the stationary steering wheel hub. Information on items like engine speed, oil pressure, battery output and fuel and coolant temperatures travels from various sources via fibre optics to the LCD display which has three fluorescent tubes constructed from several layers of different elements to give the best visual

Main picture The Wildcat at speed looks purposeful with its forward driving position and its mid-mounted engine covered by a separate bodywork panel. It follows the Bertone Athon style of five years before with an anonymous flat-back appearance
Inset The bubble-like canopy hinges forward for access to the cockpit. Doors, it seems, are still as much out of favour with futuristic design as they ever were

results. The steering wheel itself rotates around its hub on a planetary gear arrangement. An ingenious feature of the display protects the recorded mileage of the car and should some unscrupulous dealer ever attempt to 'clock' such a car, the display will show ERROR as a tribute to his deceit. Perhaps the highlight of the information sources is the Head Up Display (HUD) located on the top surface of the dashboard. This projects an image on to a transparent screen, 51 inches (130cm) from the driver's eyes and in his line of sight, and indicates speed and gear.

There is a vast array of other information available to the driver, including an indicator for front, rear and lateral G force, a tyre slippage graph for an indication of slippage during acceleration and deceleration, instantaneous horsepower and torque curves and a three-dimensional map of the spark function that shows the spark output for precise state of tune of the engine working from three variables. This provides the performance-conscious driver with everything he needs and more. Care has been taken not to allow this technology to detract from

the driver's enjoyment in exercising a high degree of individual control.

Such a combination of design, engineering and electronics is rarely seen in competitive production cars but the Wildcat marks a direction that the Buick Motor Division of GM will continue to pursue. PPG Industries Inc. (see page 60), which in recent years has initiated this and other concept cars for its PPG Pace Car Series which accompanies many of the Indy-type races in the USA, gives the public the chance to see the Wildcat in action – one beast that will not be tamed!

M4S

DODGE

Like the Buick Wildcat (see pages 54-9), the Dodge M4S is the product of collaboration between a leading American motor manufacturer and PPG Industries Inc. PPG, which has been supplying paint to the Detroit car giants for many years, created a new concept in product endorsement when it introduced its PPG Pace Car Series. Rather than spending directly on advertising, it

put up a percentage of the development costs in conjunction with major manufacturers for a number of one-off vehicles. These cars take turns to lead the field as pace cars in the Indy Car World Series and PPG and the manufacturers thus gain exposure at the beginning of every race and whenever the pace car has to be called out, while the manufacturer acquires a highly sophisticated research project for a fraction of the normal cost.

With the Wildcat, Buick opted for an amalgamation of technologies, but Dodge was after one thing – speed. And speed is what it has achieved. In early tests at the 7½-mile (12-km) oval circuit at Ohio's Transportation Research Center, the M4S reached a terminal velocity of 194.8mph (313.5kph) with the magic 200mph (322kph) mark looming large on the horizon.

Several factors enable the M4S to set its sights on this speed, the major ones being its engine and aerodynamics. The power unit is a highly developed version of Chrysler's evergreen 2.2-litre, four-cylinder unit which is mounted transversely behind the driver.

Extracting 440bhp from such a small engine required some pretty sophisticated engineering from Cosworth which also powers the

Indy cars led by the M4S at the start of every race. Its input comes in the form of a 16-valve alloy cylinder head and extra muscle is derived from a pair of inter-cooled Garrett T-25 turbochargers blowing at 23psi, an enormously high pressure for anything but a racing engine which in effect this has become.

Fuel to match the demands of this thirsty engine is delivered through twin Bosch L-Jetronic electronically managed fuel-injection systems which ensure optimum flow at all times. Transmitting all this power through a production transaxle could be problematic, so the Chrysler five-speed unit with its spur gears has been beefed up and fitted with an oil pump and oil-cooler.

Big horsepower outputs are nothing new to American machinery. The muscle cars of the Sixties had them by the shovel-full, but the Dodge M4S also excels in wind-cheating aerodynamics. With a windscreen raked to 73 degrees, flowing body-lines and integrated spoilers, the car achieves the phenomenally low drag coefficient of just 0.236.

The design of the M4S dates back to 1983 when PPG and Chrysler (the mother company of Dodge) collaborated in the design of a car for the Pace Car Series. Chrysler's designers were led by Bob Ackerman, Manager of the Product Design Office, and took their inspiration from World Endurance Championship and IMSA GTP racing cars, all of which bear the characteristic short front overhang and long rear tail section that the M4S continues.

Development was sub-contracted to a firm which worked closely with

the Computer Aided Design group from Chrysler's design offices to produce a body from styrofoam. When complete, a cast was made from which the final moulds for the glass fibre panels could be taken.

The meeting place for mechanical and body parts is a Huffaker-modified tubular racing car chassis. In

Dodge was after one thing — speed. And that is what it has achieved, reaching a terminal velocity of 195mph (314kph)

fact, body and chassis met first for the car's aerodynamic efficiency to be put to the test in the wind-tunnel where the 0.236 Cd was established. Obviously, in full Pace Car regalia, the M4S would not be as clean, as fittings like the roof-mounted light box and windscreen wipers would have to be added.

Downforce for stability at the velocities which this car is capable of attaining is provided by adjustable

Left The Chrysler rival to the GM Buick Wildcat is the Dodge Charger. There is less style but more practicality with conventional instrumentation
Above The Dodge's power unit is a highly tuned turbo four which pushes the car to a top speed approaching 200mph (322kph)

wings at the rear between the extended fenders and at the front within the grille aperture. Additionally, this opening at the front and the skirts running the length of the car between the 16 × 9-inch (41 × 23cm) BBS alloy wheels, generate 'ground effect' to suck the car to the ground.

Naturally, as in any racing machine, safety has played a large part in the design and the M4S is fully equipped to racing specification to afford the 'pilot' the best chance of survival in the event of a mishap.

The driver's environment itself is finished in quality with leather upholstery; externally, the finishing touch was naturally applied by PPG who painted the panels in basic PPG black. This was then glossed with 16 coats of pearl and five coats of clear lacquer to create a finish that 'glows' golden brown to mauve depending on the light and allows the Dodge M4S concept car to slip smoothly through the air.

The stylists have done an excellent job with the Dodge M4S for, as well as being remarkably sleek, it has an aggressive look with plenty of identity. In the thickest crowd it would attract the eye

From being one of the more conservative American car companies, Dodge has moved to the forefront of technology and style with the M4S. It is doubtful whether it, or even a close derivative will ever see production, but the ideas tested out on it are sure to filter through to the company's range over the coming years.

EXCALIBUR

The Excalibur began life in 1951 when the Beassie Engineering Corporation was established in Milwaukee, Wisconsin. It was intended as a simple, easy-to-maintain, competition car to be built in quite small quantities for the growing amateur racing formula administered by the Sports Car Club of America (SCCA).

Designated model J, the car was based on the chassis and engine from the Henry J saloon car made by the huge Kaiser-Frazer Corporation in

BUR

their Willow Run plant in Michigan. Henry Kaiser made his millions from refrigeration before the Second World War, and then turned his production over to making bombers for the United States Army Air Force. After 1945 he converted his giant factory to making automobiles for the car-starved population of North America. His model J came in two engine sizes, but it was the 2.6-litre six-cylinder version that provided Beassie with the basis for its racing car, although the Kaiser engine was hard put to develop more than 85bhp.

The Excalibur model J was a sports/racing car, as this was the type of machine most of the SCCA races catered for, and three prototypes were made. The car's bodywork was styled by Brooks Stevens, a young and very promising industrial designer, and was the car's only notable feature. It was raced in 1953, still in prototype form, looking for investors willing to put money into a small production run of the car. Nobody took the bait, and in 1955 Beassie closed its doors and ceased to exist.

Nine years later, in 1964, Brooks Stevens was working out a four-year contract with the ailing Studebaker Corporation. His employers had commissioned a 'special' for the New

York Auto Show to be held in the April of that year. Stevens had visited the earlier Chicago Auto Show and come away depressed by what he had seen on the Studebaker stand. The company's products were quite simply very, very dull and were not attracting buyers by virtue of this simple fact. He decided that what was needed was a spectacular 'special', and found inspiration in the shape of the 1928 Mercedes-Benz 38/250 SSK sports car.

Stevens ordered a Studebaker Lark Daytona convertible with its 289-cubic inch (4.7-litre) V8 engine, independent front suspension, and front disc brakes, and with his two sons, David and William, set about creating his show 'special'. In a remarkably short six weeks the car was finished and ready for transporting to New York. But Stevens hadn't accounted for the Studebaker management, who staged an about-

Previous pages The Excalibur re-creates the Thirties with its Mercedes-Benz SSK pastiche looks. It has every bit of the presence of its illustrious forebear

Above and right A detached trunk for the luggage and a decorative spare-wheel cover hint at days long gone. The radiator bears an Arthurian sword

face on the project after seeing it. They declared that the Stevens contemporary classic would clash with the company's image as a maker of 'common-sense' cars, and they refused to sponsor it!

Convinced that he had a winner, Stevens, at his own expense, took an independent stand at the show, and put his car on display. It was a sensational success, proclaimed 'The Hit of the Show'.

Freeing himself from the Studebaker contract, Stevens, in partnership with his sons, founded the SS Automobiles company, and located it in the old Beassie factory. He stayed with the Lark Daytona convertible chassis which, being narrower than other manufacturers' chassis units, was perfect for the vintage styling of the Stevens body. It also allowed the driver to put all the 290bhp developed by the V8 on to the road with some security, aided by the disc brakes and independent front suspension. Some chassis re-engineering had to take place, but that was a simple enough matter, and by 1966 Stevens had made and sold 100 copies of his Excalibur SSK.

Stevens had always insisted that only the best of materials and workmanship should be used in his creation, and as much as any other feature of the car it was this adherence to quality that secured the success of SS Automobiles as a specialist car-maker.

The year 1966 began with a serious blow to the Stevens operation, when the Studebaker Corporation closed the doors of its Canadian plant, the only one left to it, in Hamilton, Ontario. Brooks Stevens was forced to look elsewhere for his vital components, the engine/

Right The Excalibur's front is an interesting blend of up-to-date American safety regulations in the bumpers with the sweeping wings and gravestone-like grille of the original Mercedes

Below Let not the original style intrude too much: the Excalibur has the modern luxuries which its buyers deem necessities. There is automatic transmission and air-conditioning too

The Excalibur has provided many people with wind-in-the-hair motoring; maintained a reputation for sound workmanship and the use of good materials; and remains a unique car with real image

transmission and chassis. He found what he wanted within the Chevrolet division of the General Motors Corporation. Here he bought the 300bhp Corvette V8 engine, one of the greatest engines ever designed, a 327-cubic inch (5.3-litre) power house that developed 300bhp. He also bought the chassis of the Corvette, and many suspension and brake components for his new Series Two Excalibur that was to go on sale in late 1969.

A delectable option for the speed-mad Excalibur owner was the 435bhp Paxton super-charger-equipped model. For this car the new Corvette all-disc braking set-up soon proved to be a heaven-sent safety feature! Powered by this engine, Stevens claimed that his SSK would cover the 0–60mph (0–97kph) dash in less than 5 seconds (a 2-second improvement over the 289 Studebaker power-unit), and would have a top speed of over 155mph (249kph)! This latter figure is optimistic; even with the full 435bhp of the blown engine, the bluntly styled Excalibur must have been struggling to come within 20mph (32kph) of that claim.

When the Series Two car was put through its paces by America's

EXCALIBUR

motoring press it received universal praise for its on-the-road behaviour. Ride, roadholding, steering and braking, allied to the car's light 2,700lb (1,215kg) all-up weight, were complimented as much as the performance from the new engine. The Excalibur was stated to be a car worth considering in its own right, rather than just a pale copy of a classic car.

Along with the new car's mechanical components, Stevens was now able to offer many options to give each customer an individual car. These items included full air-conditioning (even for an open car!); a heater and windscreen demister; variable power-assisted steering; a tilting steering wheel; Posi-Traction limited-slip rear axle; AM-FM radio; Turbo-Hydramatic automatic transmission; leather seats; twin side-mounted spare wheels; a hard-top; self-levelling rear shock absorbers, and so on.

Together with the SSK, Stevens introduced two more models: a more luxurious roadster, the SS, and a phaeton four-seater aimed at the family driver. Prices were £8,200 for the SSK, £8,500 for the SS, and £8,850 for the phaeton.

Although the early Stevens-made Excaliburs had alloy, hand-beaten bodies glass fibre very soon became standard for all subsequent cars. Stevens used expensive, aircraft-quality material and even bought his headlights from a major French manfacturer. His car's instruments were classical white-on-black dials, and they were mounted in an engine-turned dashboard panel.

From its introductory price of £5,100 the Excalibur increased in price by nearly 100 per cent in four years. It also put on 400lb (181kg) in weight. The original car, with its cycle wings, was quite acceptable to European eyes, but with the 1970 models the car was beginning to look a little gross. It continued to sell in large numbers in the USA, however, where its unique appearance, performance and build-quality ensured that there were always more customers for it than the Milwaukee plant could keep up with. The cycle-winged SSK model was phased out of production in late 1970, and although the 'Muncie' four-speed manual gearbox was the standard transmission, most buyers specified the Turbo-Hydramatic autobox! It is also interesting to know that the stark SSK with its cycle wings remains the most sought-after Excalibur, even after 20 years!

Since 1966 Excalibur has remained the number one specialist car-maker in the USA and has seen many dozens, maybe even hundreds, of copies come and go. Some of them have been even more expensive, the vast majority cheaper and nastier, but none of them has anything like the integrity and customer allegiance of Brooks Stevens's masterpiece.

FERRA

GTO

FERRARI

I f the latest Ferrari product to carry the illustrious GTO title has a fault it is probably that it resembles the 308GTB a little too much for the comfort of some of its 200 buyers who laid out £73,000 each in 1985.

In pure engineering terms, there is no real reason for the GTO's more-than-passing resemblance to the half-as-costly staple product that is produced behind the same green factory gates, particularly as the two share very few mechanical or body

parts. Certainly, the casual onlooker could be led to undervalue seriously the work of Ferrari's engineers who have designed a new and unique car in the GTO, and of Pininfarina's body designers too, who adapted the elegant and classic lines of the 308GTB to suit a chassis different in all dimensions.

Apparently, an all-new shape would have created problems: problems of time, which Ferrari did not have in copious amounts, and problems of identity. A completely fresh shape would have had to be in line with the newer Ferrari look, typified by the Mondial and Testarossa, and thus at odds with the classic idiom of track-bred Ferraris as represented by the original GTO.

Unveiled at the 1984 Geneva Motor Show, the new Ferrari GTO is the spiritual heir to the magical Ferrari 250 GTO of 1962, winner of three world Grand Touring championships in 1962, 1963 and 1964, and of numerous other events such as the 1962 Le Mans 24 hours.

GTO stands for *Gran Turismo Omologato* (homologation Grand Touring car) and the original car started life at Maranello as a direct descendent of the 250 GT Berlinetta. Its transformation from GT to GTO was due to a mistaken interpretation of a telegram to the United States, confirming the entry in a race of the 250 GTO. In this instance the final letter 'O' stood for *omologata*, Italian for 'approved' by the official organizations to compete in the GT category. This was not understood in America, where it was believed that GTO was the car's full designation.

The misunderstanding was cleared up later, but after the auspicious outcome of the race, the 'O' was kept as part of the official designation.

Apart from the name and the spirit that inspired the GTO of the Eighties, the two cars have nothing else in common. Their technologies are in every way 20 years apart, and that applied to the new car is the best and most advanced offered by a Grand Touring car today. That there were no financial constraints allowed the techniques of building Formula-One cars to apply. These are significant not so much for ingenuity, although that is not lacking, but, more importantly in a car of this nature, because they are very efficient.

Pure Formula-One techniques governed the use of Kevlar-reinforced glass fibre honeycomb in the construction of the bonnet and the bulkhead between the engine bay and the passenger compartment.

Ferrari's reinforced plastics expert is their Formula-One designer, Dr Harvey Postlethwaite, who says that the new material is strong, light and almost indestructible, with very good molecular stability which should see it unchanged in state after many years, unlike steel which rusts. The bulk of the GTO's body is glass fibre, much advanced over that used on the first 308s, and the doors, which are 308 components, are steel for ease of manufacture and because they have the side-intrusion barriers already type-approved for world markets.

Although the centre section of the GTO is identical to the 208-308GTB, the rest is totally new. The front end carries a deep front spoiler for stability at the 180mph (290kph) of which the car is said to be capable. The four rectangular lights below the bumper line supplement the normal pop-up headlamps and are used for flashing any lesser machinery you may meet as well. The bold wing-mirrors give much better rear vision than those on the GTB, but viewing the car's profile, the most eye-catching differences are the wider wings which boost the car's width by 7½ inches (19cm). They are necessary to accommodate the Goodyear Eagle NCT tyres of 225/55VR16 and 265/

Above Just the high-flying mirrors on either flank help the lay person to distinguish the GTO from its lesser stablemates. Only the centre section of the car is shared with the 328GTB, recent successor to the 308, however
Right The car's engine bay is dominated by the twin Behr inter-coolers which ensure that the intake air is dense and cool for better combustion. Underneath is a high-tech V8 engine with 400bhp at its disposal which it will readily convert into rocket-like acceleration

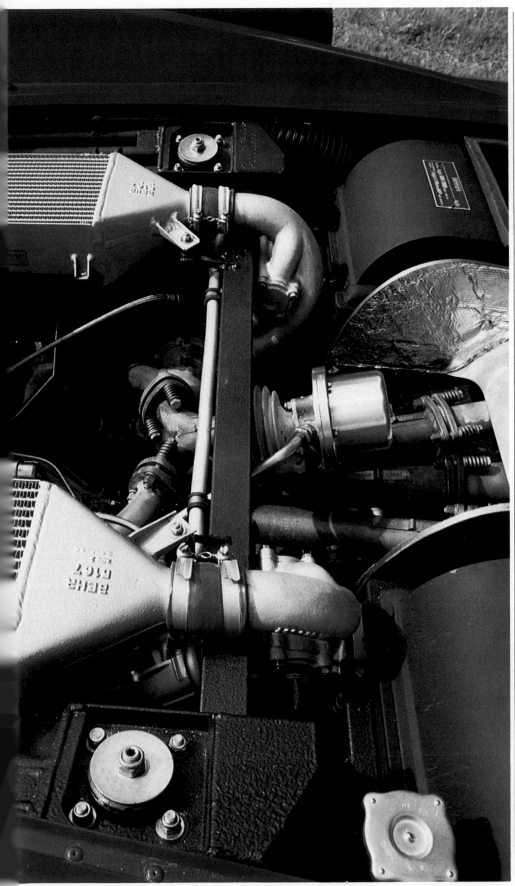

50VR16 sites, front-to-rear mounted on 8 × 16-inch (20 × 41cm) and 10 × 16-inch (25 × 41cm) Speedline three-piece alloy split-rims. The wheelbase is 4⅓ inches (11cm) longer and at the tail, an integrated spoiler generates downforce.

The one visual link with the 1962 GTO is the three slots behind the rear wheels, reminiscent of those on the front wings of the earlier car. Although they are of a different shape and position to those on the Sixties car, to aficionados they say 'GTO' even more loudly than the badge on the tail of the car.

With maximum attention to aerodynamics, numerous air intakes puhctuate the curvaceous Pininfarina body. Each opening has a very precise function: those in front serve the radiator, the air-conditioning condenser and the ventilated front disc brakes. On the flanks, they draw in air for the twin inter-coolers of the turbochargers, the oil-cooler and for engine bay ventilation. Form follows function.

Ferrari's attention to detail has also ensured the longevity of his 200 masterpieces. While there is no chance of corrosion ever attacking the bodyshell, the tubular steel space-frame chassis might be at risk from the elements, were it not for the structural plates being of Zincrox multi-layer, electro-galvanized steel.

There wasn't so much as a whisper in the GTO's brief of the four-wheel-drive, adjustable ride height, or ABS braking features that the Porsche technocrats have built into their interpretation of the homologation Grand Touring car. It is not that the engineers at Maranello are not familiar with such devices but rather that they know both that 4WD

tubular chassis is a suspension configuration that is race-bred yet conventional for a mid-engined Ferrari. Unequal-length wishbones front and rear are controlled by coil springs, Koni dampers and anti-roll bars. To keep the overall suspension height to a minimum, each front unit connects to the lower portion of its hub carrier and feeds loads into the body between the wishbone mounts. At the rear, where compactness is not so critical, the

Top and bottom left The GTO's interior is restrained and functional in typical Ferrari tradition. Closest to the driver and also on the bonnet is the badge displaying the black, prancing stallion on a golden background – the colour of the coat of arms of Enzo Ferrari's native Modena

systems do not have the adjustability of on-the-limit handling that racing drivers need for circuit use and that ABS systems are similarly unsuited to racing applications because the ability to lock up the wheels, perhaps half-way through a spin, is sometimes necessary. They reason that a driver with the ability to drive a GTO on the limit would have the ability to adjust his braking to suit conditions.

Attached to the space-frame

Below If some cars are works of art, then the Ferrari GTO comes closest to being a blue-chip investment. Some cars have been delivered on the backs of transporters (driving out of the factory's gates is more usual) to be locked away in air-conditioned suspense

spring/damper assembly connects to the top of the hub carrier. In usual Ferrari fashion, rack-and-pinion steering is used and here requires 2.9 turns lock-to-lock.

There are ventilated disc brakes on all four wheels with separate servo circuits front and rear. The aluminium alloy calipers were the result of collaboration between Ferrari and Brembo, which specializes in top-notch motor cycle brakes, and the front units have twin-pot calipers

To look upon such a special car as a mere investment is to desecrate its spirit. With it, Enzo Ferrari has successfully redefined the outer limits of motoring excellence

which are said to provide good initial bite. The handbrake acts on the rear wheels.

While none of the chassis components is anything but a logical development from past Ferraris, the

highlight of the car, the engine, is entirely new. The 2,855cc, 90-degree, V8, alloy, dry-sumped engine is based on the production 3-litre, 4-cam, 32-valve unit, as used in the 308 and Mondial. Mounted longitudinally the GTO engine benefits from strengthening of castings, uprated cooling and oil circulation and is capable of producing 400bhp at 7,000rpm and 366lb ft of torque at 3,800rpm thanks to a pair of Japanese-made IHI turbochargers, one for each bank of cylinders, each with its own Behr inter-cooler. The boost pressure is 11.6 psi, enforced by a wastegate valve, and blows into Weber-Marelli fuel-injection which is also split into two banks and linked to the breakerless ignition systems by a computer 'black box'. Cooling is by a 22-litre radiator with twin fans.

In racing trim, boost increases can unfetter a further 200bhp from the GTO's power unit with ease. The five-speed gearbox is arranged in line with the engine and is a race-derived unit built in-house with a magnesium-aluminium housing.

The sum of £73,000 was required for each of the 200 GTOs which could top 189mph (304kph), accelerate from 0–60mph (0–97kph) in 4.7 seconds and complete the standing kilometer (⅝ mile) in 21.8 seconds. Such exclusivity is an instant gold mine for the makers and a gilt-edged investment for those lucky enough to acquire one of these cars. But to look upon such a special Ferrari in this manner is to desecrate the spirit of the GTO, a spirit that the men at Maranello have carried faithfully across two decades to redefine the outer limits of motoring excellence.

The Pininfarina-designed GTO is a modern classic, combining perfectly sensuous curves, practicality and Ferrari charisma. The basic 308 design has been around for well over a decade but it has not aged at all in that time, and the baby Ferraris are still the epitome of top-class sports-car design

HOOPE

BENTLEY TURBO R
HOOPER

T he Hooper Coachbuilding Company has a history of making custom-built coach bodies dating back to the early nineteenth century. Its involvement with automotive work dates from 1907, when it formed an association with the young Rolls-Royce company. Until fairly recently car-makers like Rolls-Royce built their cars without the bodies, many customers preferring to take the running chassis to an independent coachbuilder for a one-off body design to be made and fitted to their particular specification. Supplying this rich and exclusive

The interior of the Hooper Bentley exudes an aura of luxury and comfort. To travel far and fast in this car is a pleasure rivalling that of the private jet

market was Hooper's niche in the commercial world. It was conservative in styling and pre-eminent in craftmanship. Quiet good taste, in the British manner, was, and still is, its trademark. Its cars were in use the world over by statesmen, diplomats, stars of the stage and silver screen, captains of industry, and by members of the royal families of both Great Britain and other countries. The

silent Rolls-Royce, with its distinctive body and luxurious interior displaying fine leathers, veneered wood trim, and the best Wilton carpeting, carried the name (and fame) of the Hooper company into motor-houses in nearly every part of the civilized world, even into the Kremlin where Vladimir Ilich Ulyanov (Lenin) and Joseph Stalin loved the car. Since the early Thirties Rolls-Royce have also owned the Bentley name.

After the Second World War the trade in these expensive specialist car bodies gradually faded away, with many of the great names in custom

Hooper has carried out the most minor changes on the Bentley Mulsanne Turbo R, including small side skirts and NACA ducts set into the elegant bonnet. Wheel trims are new, as is the grille

coachbuilding ceasing to exist. The list of the great companies that are no longer in business is endless: James Young of Bromley, which closed its doors in the Fifties, Thrupp and Maberly, Van den Plas which died away in 1979, Gurney Nutting, Barker, Freestone and Webb, H.J. Mulliner and so on. Until five or six years ago Hooper was in some danger of following its competitors down this path, but a timely injection of money and some dynamic new leadership have seen this old-established house not only come back from the dead, but go on to far greater things.

Still very closely and exclusively tied to the Rolls-Royce company, Hooper is busier today than ever before. Since 1981, its small North London works has expanded to three times its previous size and the workforce has doubled. It no longer makes complete bodies, mainly because the base Rolls-Royce car now has a monocoque body, and the lack of a separate chassis makes life impossible for the complete body-maker. Hooper carries out extensive body re-shaping, and in the words of the chief executive, Colin Hyams, 'We make a better silk purse out of a good silk purse!' The trim, leatherwork, and wood detailing are still to the highest standards, and new and exciting finishes have been developed in one or two areas. Even with four to six months required for finishing each car, and a very high cost per vehicle, Hooper's products remain in demand with customers from all parts of the world.

At the 1986 Geneva Automobile Show which, as the first major international show of each year, attracts the best work of all the great

manufacturers, Hooper displayed two of its finest cars, with its Bentley two-door Turbo R sports saloon hogging the limelight.

Based on the Mulsanne Turbo R (priced at £72,000), Hooper adds over £53,000 worth of extra attraction, to make the final price a nice round £125,000 on delivery! What does the lucky buyer get for all this extra cost? The first thing that Hooper does is to remove all the body paint and carry out several small but important changes to the front and rear of the body. New paint, selected by the customer to be exclusive to him/her, is applied in many coats to give the special exclusive-to-Hooper finished look. The Geneva Show car comes in 'Royal Blue', a deep, dark blue with a pearlescent undercoat. Small side skirts and front and rear spoilers, all

Left The mighty turbocharged Rolls-Royce V8 engine delivers dynamic forward thrust with as little fuss as would a giant electric motor

Below The colour-coded radiator-grille surround signifies that the car's power plant is turbocharged

Far left It is hard to believe that Hooper can improve on the already top-class finish of the standard Bentley, but improve on it, it certainly does with a really sumptuous interior **Top and bottom left** Both interior and exterior are immaculately finished

made in alloy (glass fibre, the common material, is not for Hooper!) and quite superbly styled, are matched to the body colour, and together with the body changes give the car a strong shape, making it look smaller and much faster than the base car. The radiator grille slats are exchanged for a wire mesh design. The bonnet top is provided with air intakes in the fashion of NACA-ducts to aid engine-compartment-cooling. Chromed alloy wheels of a very exclusive design, with the 'B' for Bentley cast into their centre sections, and an electrically operated sliding

steel sunroof complete the outside look of the car.

Inside we find the usual Hooper fine craftsmanship on display. The seats are electrically adjustable with a 'position memory', and front and back are covered in the finest hides. Veneered wood covers the door capping rails and instrument dash panel. A four-spoke steering wheel has its rim covered in the same leather as the seats, and its spoke colour matches the body colour. The centre console has a full range of radio/stereo hi-fi equipment of the latest design, and incorporates a compact disc player; a cellular telephone comes as standard.

The Hooper Bentley Turbo R is as swift as it is beautiful. A top speed of 132mph (212kph) and acceleration from 0–60mph (0–97kph) in 6.7 seconds is fast by any standards, and is provided by the turbocharged V8 engine which develops 298bhp at 4,600rpm. The chassis is uprated to complement this fine engine.

The Hooper Bentley Turbo R stands supreme in its class and it is an indication of the excellence of this car to note that the only criticism that any of the motoring press could level concerned the lack of an anti-lock braking system in the car's design. Typically, Rolls-Royce has announced that it is 'investigating' this feature for possible use in future models!

SPYDER 033i
AND IMPERATOR 108i

ISDERA

In 1978, after seven years at the drawing-board with Porsche in Stuttgart, gifted German car designer Eberhard Schulz left with the drawings for his dream car in his briefcase. Like so many designers in the German motor industry at that time, the car he

A

idolized was the classic Mercedes 300SL Gullwing, and the CW311 Project, as he named it, was his interpretation of an Eighties version of that car. Fortune brought together Schulz and Rainer Buchmann of b + b in Frankfurt and their meeting enabled Schultz to complete the

half-finished prototype secreted in his Stuttgart garage.

Built to be the ultimate road-going sports car, the CW311's chassis was of tubular frame design and used double wishbone suspension at all four corners in typical competition-car style. The glass fibre bodywork

naturally featured gullwing doors and a huge, steeply raked windscreen with a single, very long wiper. The meatiest power unit available at the time was the Mercedes-Benz 6.9-litre V8; AMG waved its magic wand over this 286bhp power unit to bring its output up to 370bhp and it was then installed amidships in the CW311. Needless to say, performance is quite staggering: the car will reach 100mph (161kph) in only 7.8 seconds from a standing start and tops out at 198mph (319kph) which is achieved, we are told, after only another 14 seconds!

Rear vision hardly matters; after all, what could possibly catch you? None the less, a periscope-type rear-view device supplements the small rear window. There are no door mirrors to spoil the drag factor.

Schulz's talents were not confined to pure car designing, though, and in 1979, the same year that he designed the Porsche 928 Cabrio and Targa for b + b (see pages 26-33), he evolved the famous Pirelli P-wheel design for the German division of that tyre-maker. This has since been adopted by Volkswagen for its Golf GTi. Later that year, Schulz also developed the directional aero-wheel for b + b. Then he and b + b parted company and he spent the next two years working on the BMW Futuro, the Sauber C6 Group C racing car and the fairings for the WM-Kreidler racing motor cycle.

Previous pages The parachute is not standard issue, but a pair of silver flying suits with matching crash helmets come as part of the Spyder package

In 1982, eager to make his own mark in the car-manufacturing world as well as bringing to fruition what he knew were his best designs, Schulz established Isdera, acronym for the bilingual Ingenieurbüro für Styling, Design and Racing.

The first of the new company's projects was the 033i Spyder, a topless runabout that appeals to people with a large helping of *joie de vivre* – not to mention money. This £20,700 (in 1982) 'four-wheeled motor cycle' is the sort of car you go out for a blast in on warm sunny days, so to make up for the lack of protection from the weather, the package includes a pair of silver driving suits and full-face crash helmets to match. This must be the closest experience to low flying for two available!

In overall concept, apart from its modern, mid-engined configuration, the 033i Spyder has strong evidence of the Porsche 550 Spyder, yet another of Schulz's Sixties dream cars, even down to the silver paint that graced most of the Porsches leaving the factory. Like some Porsches of

Left The Isdera Imperator in its earlier incarnation as the b + b CW311. There have been minor changes to the design in its lifetime, and the Isdera version no longer boasts the Mercedes-Benz three-pointed star on its grille

Right, top and bottom The Isdera Spyder takes the idea of a pure roadster one stage further than cars like the Caterham 7. Even though it has no hood, the Spyder still has sophisticated cant-forward doors. A crash helmet is an integral part of driver weather protection

days gone by, the 033i uses VW parts in its mechanical make-up. The most powerful compact engine available in 1982 was the VW Golf GTi unit and Schulz sent this 1.8-litre fuel-injected engine along to the famous tuner Dr Schrick, who raised the power output to 136bhp through his usual cylinder-head and camshaft modifications. This being the 'cooking' version, Isdera also offered a warmed-over, 250bhp, turbocharged, five-cylinder Audi 200 Turbo power unit for another £5,900. The gearbox was drawn from the Porsche 924 Turbo and, with the shortest final drive that he could find to compensate for a tall fifth gear, Schulz was able to claim a 6.8-second 0–60mph (0–97kph) time and an average of 31mpg (11km per litre) for the Golf GTi-engined version. Since the car has neither roof nor windscreen, top speed is academic, but handling is of paramount importance. Formula-One-like forward seats thus balance the mechanicals to give an ideal 50/50 weight distribution when the driver is alone.

While the rear luggage compartment lid is released from inside the cockpit, removal of the engine cover requires a screwdriver. It is surprising how much room you will then find for access to normal servicing areas. The gearbox and differential are placed behind the engine and are reached from below.

The chassis beneath the glass fibre bodyshell is a classic triangulated mixture of round and square tubing in a space-frame arrangement. Suspension is coil-over-shock MacPherson strut all round with extra radius rods (ex-Porsche) at the rear, while steering comes from the

The Isdera package includes a pair of silver driving suits and full-face crash helmets to match. This must be the closest experience to low flying for two available!

Porsche 911. Brakes are the latest floating caliper ATE units with discs all round. The alloy wheels are 6 × 15 inch (15 × 38cm) and of the Pirelli P-wheel design that Schulz created three years previously and these are shod with 195/50VR15 P7 tyres.

The front-hinged doors on their gas struts give a futuristic touch to the act of entering the car; this is best done by bracing your hand on the back of the special Recaro seats and lowering your legs into the narrow footwell, which may take some

Right The central instrument console of the Spyder is courtesy of an Opel saloon, while the large, central rev-counter indicates the sporting nature of the beast

practice. Passengers have a slight advantage, as the glove box assembly lifts up with the door.

Once installed in the driver's seat, you view the curved dashboard through a leather-bound Nardi steering wheel. The rev counter is dead ahead and the speedometer, clock, switches and integrated rearview mirror are set at an angle in mid dash, while the minor gauges for oil pressure, water temperature, fuel and volts angle in from a plinth on the lift-up driver's door.

Above The Spyder lines up next to the more lavish Imperator, which offers a little more protection from the weather

As a one-man band, Schulz is able to progess very quickly and since he launched his Isdera 108i Imperator in 1984, ties with Mercedes-Benz have been strengthened, with engine sourcing being steered away gradually from other manufacturers. Thus, the latest version of the 033i Spyder is known as the 033-16 and carries the Mercedes 190E 2.3-16 engine. This Cosworth-developed powerplant gives 185bhp and the Spyder now boasts a 156mph (251kph) top speed with 0–60mph (0–97kph) in 6.1 seconds. The tyre size has been increased to 205/50VR15 on 7 × 15 inch (18 × 38cm) alloy wheels to handle the extra power and the fuel tank capacity raised from 12.1 gallons (55 litres) to 17.2 gallons (78 litres). The asking price is £32,000.

Schulz's project for 1983 was to be the Roadster for Bitter, based on Opel mechanicals, but that year he was also readying his 108i Imperator for production. Literally the production version of the CW311, the 108i meant that at last Schulz has his two dream cars in production. With the latest 231bhp 5.0-litre V8 from Mercedes, the Imperator is not as fast but is much more efficient than its predecessor, and is still capable of an impressive 160mph (257kph). Of course, for those who demand the crowning glory of the 6.9-litre engine, Schulz will supply a 'luxury version' of the car for £29,600 more

The Isdera Imperator is an elegant design which could easily carry the badge of any of the Modenese supercar manufacturers. Its gullwing doors make access easy, the whole car being as practical as it is attractive

The luxury version of the Imperator 108i has racing suspension, lightweight components in the chassis and body aerodynamic aids. With its Mercedes-Benz 5.6-litre 300 bhp engine it can achieve a top speed of 185mph (298kph)

than the usual £75,500 price tag. This special car has racing suspension, lightweight components in the chassis and body aerodynamic aids, plus an interior that can be trimmed to customer wishes, but the car's *pièce de résistance* is a Mercedes-Benz 5.6-litre 300bhp engine or if you are even braver, there is a four-valve-per-cylinder version of the 5.0-litre engine giving 360bhp. This reduces the 0–60mph (0–97kph) time

to 4.6 seconds and enables a top speed of 185mph (298kph) to be reached.

When you think about it, makers like Porsche and Ferrari need a whole factory to build cars like the trend-setting Isdera 033i and 108i. But the greatest tribute to the far-sighted dreamer was the design prizes awarded to his 033i and 108i in 1984 and 1985 by the German Design Centre in Stuttgart.

Inset The Imperator, with its sleek, aerodynamic shape, reaches top speeds of 185mph (298kph)

Main picture The wrap-around console of the Imperator gives the interior an aircraft cockpit-like air. The crude gearchange gate would not get past the drawing-board stage at either Ferrari or Lamborghini, however

KOEN

FERRARI BOXER AND TESTAROSSA

KOENIG

Perhaps two or three times a year, eager motoring journalists from all round the world call up the offices of Koenig Specials near the railway station in central Munich to enquire after the latest parts available for Ferrari, Jaguar and Mercedes Specials. By far the most frantic and persistent calls concern the Ferraris and the race to be first in print with a test of the latest Koenig twin-turbo Ferrari is on once again.

If success is measured by the

number of motoring journalists making a pilgrimage to your door, then Willy Koenig ranks close to Enzo Ferrari, the maestro in Modena, who is not exactly overjoyed by what the German ex-publisher and Ferrari-lover does to his 'perfect creations'.

For entrepreneur Willy Koenig, the Ferrari connection goes back to the days when he was a successful publisher of technical, legal and commercial works. Racing was his hobby, and he competed in saloon and sports car track events in cars as diverse as a Ferrari 250GT, Ford GT40, Lola T70 and a works Abarth. In the late 1970s, he bought a Ferrari 512 Boxer as his road car and made some engine and suspension modifications which enabled him to demolish the opposition at Ferrari Owners' Club events. Club friends then asked him to perform similar tweaks for them and the business grew from there.

On the visual front, a chance meeting with designer Vittorio Strosek cemented a friendship which has turned into a lasting business relationship as well, with Strosek now designing all of Koenig's creations.

In the few years that Koenig has been in this business, he has been careful to build up an unimpeachable reputation for technical quality and reliability. Being a racing driver himself, he is only too aware of the need for components to stand up to the rigours of sustained driving at top speeds and thus only uses the best that money

Above There are only minor alterations to the Koenig Boxer's interior, just the addition of instruments which are necessary to keep the driver informed of the tuned engine's condition

Left Turbocharging boosts the Ferrari's power output to a solid 650bhp

can buy. 'I have a working partnership with the biggest German companies like BBS-Mahle, and the German offices of Pirelli and Koni,' he says. 'This way, I can be assured of the best quality and back-up.' Smaller specialist companies around Munich supply exhausts and carry out the engine and body modifications. The brakes come from the British firm, AP

A typical Koenig test programme for a new car is demanding in the extreme. TUV approval in Germany costs a whopping £29,000 and to be sure of durability, the Ferrari prototypes are hammered for almost 1,250 miles (2,000km) non-stop around Hockenheim circuit, virtually under racing conditions.
Willy Koenig describes his 512

Boxer conversion as being nearly a whole new car. "We have to alter and strengthen the gearbox and use stronger driveshafts, the suspension is changed, the engine stripped down and rebuilt using stronger low-compression pistons and twin turbochargers with water injection inter-coolers and an oil-cooler.' The inside of the car can be trimmed to customer requirements.' To improve its looks, the Boxer gets new front and rear lower sections made from GRP, together with matching side skirts. These integrate the side strakes and larger rear arches with a break line for the engine cover which has an integrated rear spoiler. Massive air intakes also dress this rear section and if you so desire, you can have the

large rear wing to complete the illusion. Filling out the huge arches are 9 × 15-inch (23 × 38cm) and 13 × 15-inch (33 × 38cm) BBS alloy wheels carrying Pirelli P7s of enormous 225/50VR15 and 345/35VR15 section, respectively.

With conventional tuning, a Koenig Boxer turns out about 450bhp, but the forced induction package is worth 650bhp, making the car good for 206mph (332kph). It can pass 60mph (97kph) in a mere 3.7 seconds from rest! The car's suspension and braking systems are suitably beefed up with special Koenig springs and uprated Koni dampers. The brake discs are to racing specification and carry four-pot calipers.

The centre of town on a busy morning is no place to be driving a turbocharged Ferrari Boxer, unless of course you feel that the envious glances more than make up for the frustrating exercise of constant gearchanging with that heavy clutch as you weave your way through the lesser machinery. And you certainly won't escape notice, with the complex grunts and howls so typical of Ferraris amplified by the freer exhaust of the Koenig car and echoing around the urban landscape.

Booting the car firmly off the line, the push in the back is stupendous and you have to snatch second gear within a fraction of a second, so quickly does the engine spin round to its 6,500 rpm red-line. It is almost as though there is a small turbocharger connected to the needle on the rev counter as well. Snatched one-to-two changes are never easy in a Ferrari, with the dog-leg first-to-second movement through the gate, and in a way this helps to preserve the clutch from brutal snatched changes. In any case it is best not to come off the throttle suddenly or you will hear the wastegates dumping all the boost and you know you have wasted precious time. Smooth, clean driving is thus the order of the day and if you have the engine well on boost in the mid-range when you come up alongside some other fast machine on the Autobahn, the chances are

Smooth, clean driving is the order of the day and when you come up alongside some other fast machine on the Autobahn, the chances are that you can leave it in your wake without too much trouble

that you can leave it in your wake without too much trouble.

Previous pages
Glass fibre panels clad the rear of Willy Koenig's Boxer to give the car more of a brutal look. The rear wing isn't for show: it provides the car with much-needed downforce at the high speeds of which it is more than capable

Above The Koenig Boxer doesn't look as aggressive from the side as it does from the rear, but it looks every inch as purposeful. Some would say the addenda detract from the Pininfarina original, but there is no denying its appeal

The Koenig variation on the Testarossa rather resembles his conversion of the Boxer. Much of the Pininfarina line which helps the standard Testarossa belie its size has been lost with the Turbo

Topping his 650bhp Boxer was no easy task, but then Willy Koenig only deals in ultimates. When the Ferrari Testarossa was unveiled in 1984, speculation began to grow as to how Koenig would alter this dramatic new Ferrari flagship.

Mechanically, the Testarossa is a close relative of the Boxer, but just as the Testarossa is one generation on from the Boxer, the Koenig car has taken a great leap forward as well. According to Koenig, his ideas for the new car take their cue from the Eighties. 'Cars of the Seventies were more angular, while today's cars pay more attention to aerodynamics and are thus smoother and more integrated.'

K O E N I G

He explains that while his new car is quite similar to its predecessor in mechanical terms, its design philosophy is quite different, owing a lot to current Group C (world championship) sports cars. Glass fibre is used for all the bodywork alterations, and these include a complete replacement section with integrated spoiler. This retains the

Willy Koenig produces some of the fastest, best-handling, best-stopping and most wicked road cars around, and his version of the Ferrari Testarossa is certainly no exception

original indicator/side light and driving-lamp cluster but the pop-up headlamps can be replaced by a

cowled-in arrangement of four rectangular units.

While obvious changes include further enlargement of the extended rear arches and the usual Koenig rear wing, the most outstanding and radical visual alteration is the removal of the horizontal strakes leading to the massive side intakes.

Under the skin, the new car uses basically the same formula as the twin-turbo Boxer that went before it, but the addition of bigger inter-coolers and a second oil-cooler has conspired to produce a magic 710bhp at 6,300rpm with 625lb ft of torque at 5,100rpm. But this is no peaky highly tuned engine. Even starting off with a cold engine and crowded roads there is real power from as low as 2,000rpm and the car is happy to pick up cleanly from 35mph (56kph) in fifth gear! Perhaps this is surprising for a car that can do 0–60mph (0–97kph) in 3.7 seconds and has a verified top speed of 210mph (338kph), but then Willy Koenig is in the business of producing the fastest, best-handling, best-stopping and most wicked road cars around.

You will pay dearly for the pleasure, though: this full-house Testarossa will cost a cool £110,000. Not that that sort of price tag would worry Koenig's well-heeled customers, who seem to stem from all walks of life. 'A Koenig Ferrari-buyer is a different sort of person from a classic Ferrari owner,' explains Willy Koenig. 'He has a different lifestyle and is perhaps more spontaneous.' Doctors, businessmen, film and pop stars – Jermain Jackson has a black Koenig Boxer – all have been captivated by the allure of a Koenig Ferrari.

Left The Testarossa ('red head') engine has four valves for each of its 12 horizontally opposed cylinders, rather than the two of its Boxer predecessor. The better breathing they impart helps the latest engine produce a gargantuan 710bhp and a maximum torque of 625lb ft, a figure which wouldn't be out of place on a large truck. With the engine's weight right over the rear wheels, traction is superb, as is acceleration

Overleaf The view that every other road-user will get of the Koenig Testarossa as it accelerates towards the horizon – generating inertial forces on its occupants of well over 1*g*. It actually accelerates forwards with a force one-and-a-half times greater than that which most cars can generate in an emergency stop

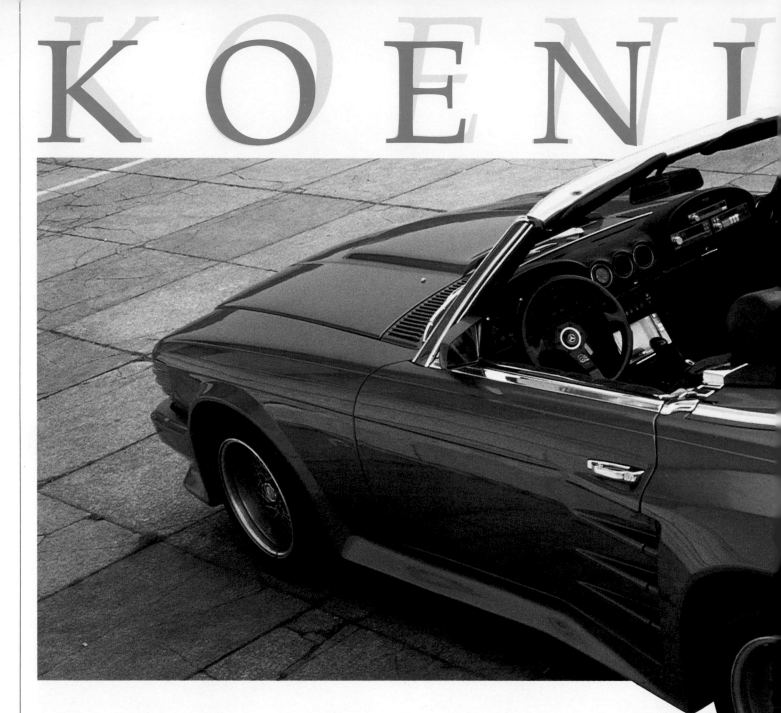

MERCEDES SL ROADSTER AND JAGUAR XJS

KOENIG

There is no motoring experience quite like the feel of the open road, with the wind in one's hair on a sunny day. Better still if it can be done in style in one of a very exclusive range of cars. Mercedes Roadsters have always been popular among the rich who have no need for a saloon car and it is that very popularity which has to some extent blunted the exclusiveness of the car. The fact that it is available with the lowly 3-litre, six-cylinder engine as well as your expensive 5-litre, V8 motor only adds salt to the wound,

G

although no customer of Koenig would dream of starting with anything less than the 5-litre.

Vittorio Strosek, Koenig's frequent partner, has been hard at work, peeling back the old-fashioned chrome and rubber bumpers of the Stuttgart-built two-seater and replacing them with integrated bumper-spoiler sections of GRP.

Flared front arches sweep down into prominent side skirts which visually explode into the Koenig trademark – side strakes and huge rear arch flares and rear spoilers.

With the black canvas hood erected, the Koenig Roadster looks rather strange, certainly more incongruous than a standard car in that configuration. Perhaps it is

because the pose value of any roadster only comes together when the hood is down and, of course, the body-styling works strongly in that direction.

But no matter – whatever you may think of the styling, this is one fast lady. True to form, Koenig has delved under the air-scoop-endowed bonnet, working an American-made Paxton supercharger into his car's specification to boost output from 231bhp to a full 320bhp at the same 4,750rpm. With the automatic

Previous pages The rear flanks of the Koenig Mercedes Roadster splay out to cover the wheels

Above The electric blue paint of the Roadster only serves to accentuate the dramatic impression it creates
Above right The rear wing ensures stability at speed
Right The Mercedes-Benz 500SL may be quite a small car, but Willy Koenig has packed comprehensive electronics into the car's interior. Witness the stereo system and television set into the centre console. Extra power is provided by a Paxton supercharger to allow *Dallas* to be watched at 160mph (258kph)!

Being an open car, it is much more likely that the gaze of envious onlookers will fall inside the 500SL's cockpit and they will find a veritable Aladdin's cave of treasures

gearbox unaltered, this shaves a full 1.5 seconds off the 0–60mph (0–97kph) time, reducing it to 6.3 seconds, and increases top speed to 160mph (258kph) where the standard car would be struggling to pass 140mph (225kph).

Once again, big wheels are needed to fill out big arches and for the SL, Koenig has chosen 9 × 15-inch (23 × 38cm) and 13 × 15-inch (33 × 38cm) BBS alloy wheels with 225/50VR15 and 345/35VR15 Pirelli P7s. All this is kept under firm rein by uprated springs and Koni dampers.

The cockpit houses a veritable Aladdin's cave of treasures. The sumptuous black-leather-clad seats, or rather armchairs, hold you in their soft clasp and help to absorb the slight harshness introduced by the huge tyres and stiffer suspension. But the stars of the show must be the audio-visual toys that occupy the dashboard and centre console. A Sony TV is buried in the centre console and its sound wafts to your ears via the multi-amped, component sound system built into the passenger's side of the dashboard, which drives an array of speakers front and rear.

Since the 500SL, Koenig and his designer Strosek have gone on to alter the 500SEC and the 500SEL. The most famous of these new 500SEC conversions belongs to Sylvester Stallone and carries the number plate 'Rocky' — something this luxury supercar certainly won't be!

Exclusivity may be a very relative thing but, at any social level, the owner of an imported car is always one up on the man with a home grown product.

There is, however, even amongst the wealthy who own cars in the Jaguar, BMW and Mercedes league, a wish to stand apart from the crowd. It is now rare to see a standard Mercedes S-Class in Germany without at least a set of alloy wheels, and the body-styling and tuning business now embraces these prestige carriages.

Although a Ferrari man at heart, Willy Koenig's commercial sense persuaded him to look at different marques as well. He set designer Vittorio Strosek to work on styling alterations that would give the car visual aggression to match the performance of its 300bhp V12 engine. The Strosek touch is unmistakable in the finished product. The rather bitty chrome bumper and chin spoiler are replaced in one fell swoop by a single bumper/spoiler unit incorporating the front indicator lights; similarly at the rear a bumper/undertray unit integrates the rear

end. The new side sills blend into the bodywork from the front arches and then sweep into the familiar side strakes that start off the huge bulging rear arch flares. A rear spoiler grows out of the top of these extended flares and is supplemented by an aerofoil mounted on the boot lid. From BBS come 8½ × 15-inch (22 × 38cm) and 11 × 15-inch (28 × 38cm) alloy wheels carrying 225/50VR15 and 285/50VR15 Pirelli P7 tyres while to stiffen things up to cope with the modified engine, Koni Sport dampers replace the factory originals.

You can retain the oval Jaguar headlamps or go for the US-type four round lamp configuration, but the airscoop on the bonnet is functional if you decide to go with the Koenig engine modifications. The more macho-looking twin exhaust pipes at the rear contribute to a 10 per cent increase in horsepower on all the engines. In standard form, the XJS can be had with either a 3.6-litre four-valve-per-cylinder straight six or the famous 5.3-litre V12. To provide V12-type performance from the smaller engine, Koenig looks to a supercharger to provide 310bhp at 5,400rpm and 322lb ft of torque at 4,100rpm. This is an increase of 40 per cent and 25 per cent respectively which endows the car with a top speed of over 150mph (241kph) and a 0–60mph (0–97kph) sprinting ability of 6.5 seconds.

The cubic capacity of the V12 allows plenty of scope for conventional tuning without loss of tractability, but Koenig prefers to start with an even larger basic capacity, so his Stage 1 conversion merits an enlargement to 5.7 litres with an exchange engine. Internal modifications include new pistons

The Koenig Jaguar has been given the visual aggression to match its performance — the ultimate conversion takes the engine out to 6.4 litres and produces a staggering 450 bhp

The familiar Koenig styling is used on the Jaguar XJS, too. Side skirts branch out into wide flanks, while a new integral nose has replaced the itemized look of the original. Whether the power unit is 3.6-litre six or 5.3-litre V12, Koenig can extract as much power as anyone could possibly desire

and a modified fuel injection system which bring output up to 380bhp. The ultimate conversion takes the engine out to 6.4 litres and produces a staggering 450bhp. Koenig uses a reinforced GM automatic transmission to convey the power and huge four-pot vented disc brakes look after retardation from the 160mph (257kph) top speed.

The car's sporty image is carried through to the interior by a pair of electrically adjustable Recaro seats and a leather-bound or wooden Momo wheel.

All this exclusivity comes at a price, though, and in Germany a complete car with a 350bhp engine costs well over £35,500. Fortunately, you do not have to buy all the parts in one go!

MAZDA

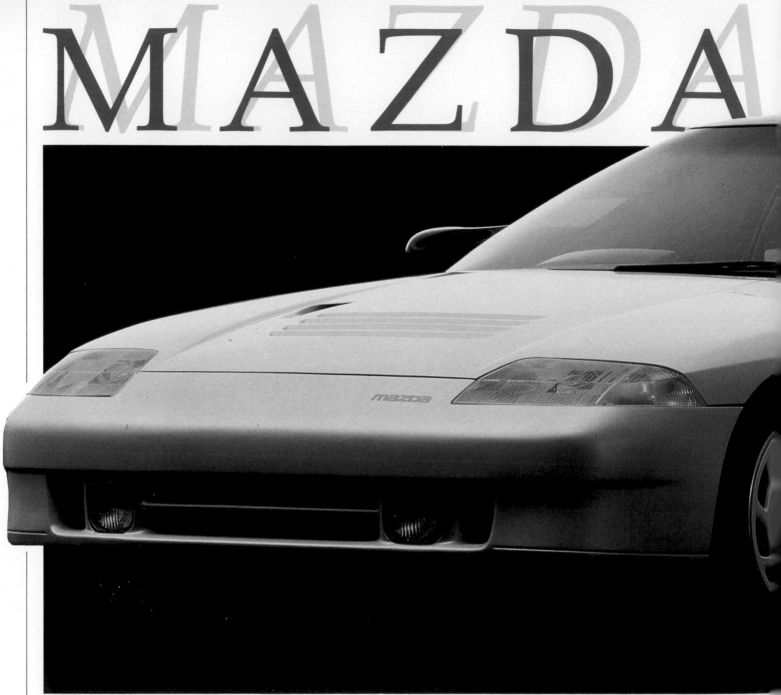

MX - 03

MAZDA

Y ou'll be amazed at a Mazda, say the company's television ads. And if you think that this Japanese manufacturer's present range of cars is impressive, then take a look at the advanced engineering that lies beneath the skin of the MX-03, Mazda's latest running concept car, which would do any major car-maker proud.

A long and low-slung sports coupé for the future, the MX-03 bears a distinctive house style. The design of its glass-house cabin in particular is strongly reminiscent of the Mazda 929 Coupé, which was sold in Japan and several European countries other

than the UK. The basic front and rear three-quarter views also strongly echo the style established by Mazda with its 929 and RX-7 models.

Under the dramatic exterior, the engineering of the MX-03 is not entirely new, but rather a logical extension of the ideas that Mazda has crystallized over the past decade in its passenger cars, as well as in the MX-02 concept car of the early Eighties. Mazda is renowned for its work on the Wankel engine concept which it developed to be an economical alternative to the reciprocating engine. Mazda's recent developments in other areas, chassis in particular, have tended to

overshadow this, but the unit installed in the MX-03 lays to rest any doubts as to the company's continuing research programme. A three-rotor adaptation of the 13B twin-rotor unit that powers the new RX-7 displaces 3 × 654cc (1,962cc) and takes the claimed engine output to 320bhp at 7,000rpm with 289lb ft of torque at 3,800rpm. These figures are achieved with the aid of turbocharging by one of the new ceramic turbine units, which possesses much better heat-dissipating qualities, fewer lubrication problems and potentially greater reliability. Coupled to this is a twin-throat intake nozzle with an

electronically controlled butterfly valve that closes one throat at low speeds to enhance the turbocharger's operation and thus low-speed response, while both throats are allowed to open at higher engine speeds so that full power can be developed. With a Cd of only 0.25, this slippery car has a calculated top speed in the region of 186mph (299kph) with 0–60mph (0–97kph) in around 5 seconds.

While the car has not been formally performance-tested, the powerplant has been earmarked for Mazda's Group C endurance racing contender. Although the MX-03 prototype engine carries ancillaries such as air-conditioning and power steering, it also has dry-sump lubrication. The Group C car may see service in 1986, but the production possibilities of the engine are as yet some way off. The complex construction of the two-piece eccentric shaft that allows assembly of the middle rotor, and the as yet unfinalized ceramic rotor tip seals and ceramic rotor inserts in combustion chamber hot spots are cited as reasons.

The project was initiated in 1984 as a sequel to the four-wheel-steering MX-02. Since 1980, Mazda has been paying considerable attention to the steering effect of the rear wheels of a car as it negotiates a corner. While certain improvements were pioneered by Porsche on the 928 series, in the form of the 'Weissach' rear end that compensates for toe effect as the car is cornered, it was Mazda who introduced the concept at the lower end of the market. Mazda reasoned that rather than merely compensating passively for toe effect, the rear wheels could be used actively to help the car take corners better at high speeds. The MX-02 used a fairly straightforward and constantly applied system of turning the rear wheels. The MX-03 has refined that system with speed-sensitive automatic variation. At low speeds, the rear wheels steer in the opposite direction from the front ones for a reduced turning circle. As road speed rises, however, the counter-steering from the rear diminishes until all assistance is removed. This happens at 25mph (40kph) and from this point on, the rear wheels turn in the same direction as the front ones,

Previous pages There is a surprising amount of the RX7 and 929 about the Mazda MX-03's look, even though the styling exercise is a lot larger. Flush-fit glass and integrated spoilers front and rear help the aerodynamics, but overall the car still looks more like a production car than many styling exercises which take their concepts too far for comprehension

Main picture and insets Careful attention has been paid to make sure that there are no edges of the body jutting into the airstream, while much thought has been applied to the overall design to ensure that the MX-03 slips easily through the air. It does so with a drag coefficient of 0.25, fully 10 per cent better than any production car

enhancing directional stability. The 15-degree maximum rear steering angle of the MX-02 has also been cut to a more modest 6 degrees, again with stability in mind.

In concert with speed-sensitive, four-wheel steering, the MX-03 also has speed-sensitive, variable-ratio steering. This uses electronics to monitor vehicle speed and vary both the effective steering ratio as well as the amount of power assistance. Thus, at low speeds, only minimal steering movements are required, while the numerical ratio of turns also grows as speed rises. Because the steering wheel need never be moved in the great arcs that characterize conventional steering, the MX-03 driver is able to direct the car via an aircraft-type grip.

Four-wheel drive has become *de rigueur* for today's very high performance cars. In the MX-03, torque split is handled along with the front/rear differential effect by a wet multi-plate clutch for each axle. Electronically controlled hydraulic valves vary the pressure coupling the clutch plates and allow total modulation between full front- to full rear-wheel drive. While other manufacturers like Audi and Ford

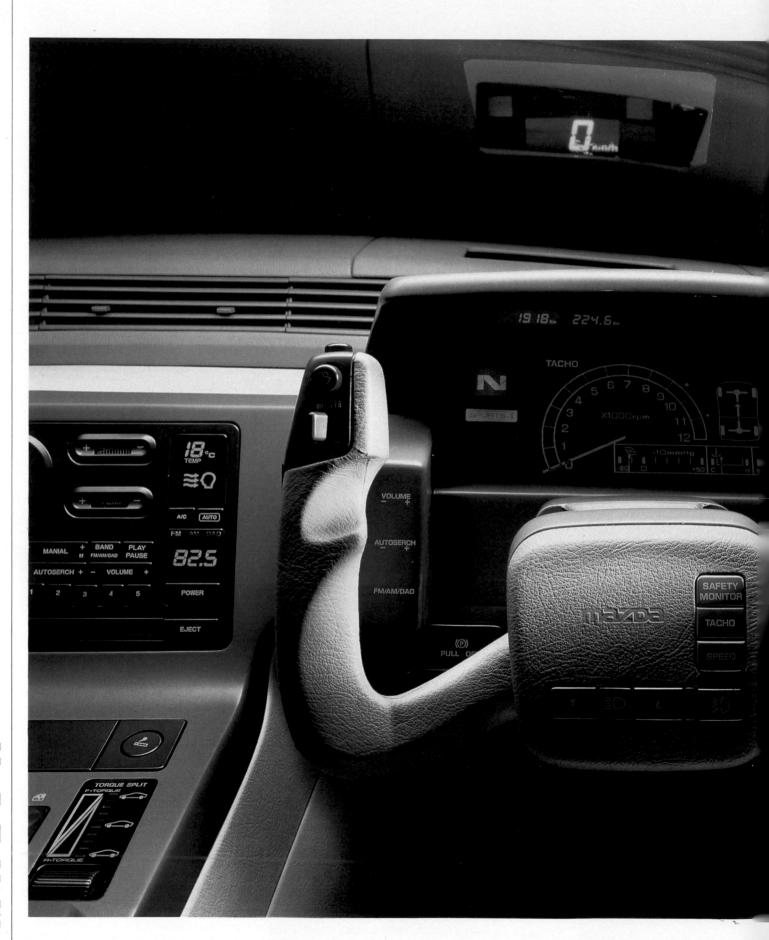

work on either a 50:50 or 34:66 per cent split, Mazda stresses that the MX-03's system is purely experimental and that in practice it would not expect more than 30 to 50 per cent of the torque to be fed to the front. Despite all the other automation, a manual torque split control is seen as an advantage as it gives the enthusiast driver the chance to select a torque split to suit his preference.

showing speed in large digits projected on the windscreen and a multi-function display with a large circular analogue tachometer. If you prefer, you can choose a more conventional display. The steering handlebar incorporates some of the more frequently used switchgear, the rest being within fingertip reach on the instrument housing. The centre of the dashboard contains the

Far left Although electronics are used to good effect for the instrumentation, the Mazda designers have gone overboard and used an aircraft-style grip and a head-up instrument display which has often proved impossible to read safely

Left Access to the interior is aided by wing-like flaps in the roof which rise when the doors are opened

If you think that Mazda's present range of production cars is impressive, take a look at the advanced engineering beneath the skin of the MX-03

This part of the system has not yet been perfected and the select lever on the prototype is only a dummy. Once again, the car is fitted with a contemporary active safety feature in the form of ABS anti-lock braking.

The interior appointments of the Mazda's latest high-tech showcase do nothing if not mirror the avant-garde engineering of the mechanicals. Trimmed in white to match the exterior, the cockpit of the car features a cross-section of all the latest display technology, with a holographic 'head-up' display

audio system and air-conditioning controls.

Like all concept cars, the Mazda MX-03 bears much that could be developed quickly for the showrooms, along with a lot of other things requiring further development work. Mazda brought four-wheel steering to the forefront with the MX-02 and has developed it into a credible system, but problems still remain for the driver of this high-tech machine. Could technology perhaps be advancing beyond human needs?

PKD 156S

DE VILLE
PANTHER

Looking down the long bonnet of a Panther De Ville from an elevated position in the driving seat, it is easy to understand how the owners of vintage Rolls-Royces and Mercedes were able to cock a snook at the rest of the populace as they glided past. Cocooned in the leather-, wood- and wool-lined cabin, a sense of lofty superiority develops very easily.

To the untrained eye, the Panther De Ville may appear to hail from the Thirties, with its tall, chrome-plated grille on the end of a long bonnet and narrow upright body

sandwiched between curved fenders and running boards. Even a set of chromed wire wheels add to the illusion, but this is no well-preserved vintage limousine, not even a lovingly restored example. The De Ville is an exponent of the replica vintage car era *circa* 1974 and its spiritual home is Byfleet rather than Crewe or Stuttgart. But perhaps that is heritage enough, for Byfleet's claim to fame lies in the famous Brooklands racing circuit, where all the worthy machinery of those illustrious days met in anger.

In a world full of sleek, modern, executive expresses, the desire to stand out from the rest of the wealthy crowd must be overpowering, hence the sudden proliferation of body-styling and coachbuilding based on Jaguar, BMW and Mercedes cars. But for some, nostalgia is their driving force, and it was these customers with a yearning for an individual, hand-crafted motor car, with a presence that no contemporary production car can give, who enabled Panther eventually to turn out 100 of these bespoke automobiles.

After six years of producing the De Ville and also getting a small, two-seater sports car, the Lima, under way, the parent company, Panther Westwinds, went into receivership and was bought lock, stock and barrel by the South Korean-based multinational, Jindo Industries. At that point, no-one could hazard a guess as to what would become of the Byfleet-based company. There was, after all, a great distance separating Seoul and Surrey!

Six years on, the renamed and revitalized Panther Car Company has not only dispelled any doubts about the intentions of the Korean parent, led by Young C. Kim, but has also carved itself a significant niche in the British specialist sports-car market

with the Kallista, a heavily reworked and updated version of the Lima, and the dramatically styled, mid-engined Panther Solo powered by the turbocharged Cosworth Sierra engine.

Although only 100 cars were produced by the two companies between 1974 and 1985, not all Panther De Villes were born equal. While the cost of this hand-made car rose commensurate with the rate of inflation from a basic price of £35,000 to £100,000 within a decade, the final figure on your banker's draft would depend very much on the

In a world full of sleek, modern executive expresses, the desire to stand out from the rest of the wealthy crowd is overpowering. The Panther De Ville, with its mobile-gin-palace aesthetics, fits the bill perfectly

Previous pages Whereas the Excalibur is based on the Mercedes-Benz SSK, the Panther De Ville is styled on another great from the same era, the Bugatti Royale, of which just a handful of examples were built. Most Panthers were fitted with Jaguar six-cylinder engines, but a few were equipped with V12 power units

specification you dreamed up. The only car to be made in 1984, for instance, was a special six-door version for Prince Sulaiman of Selangor in Malaysia. This car was also widened and included enough extras to bring the price sticker up to £140,000. The 99th and 100th cars, made in 1985, were a pair of two-

Main picture The narrow Panther De Ville is quite cramped inside but it hasn't stopped the company squeezing as many luxurious appointments into the cabin as possible
Inset Leather and wood veneer are used to the full, while the carpet is naturally thick and sumptuous

door cars, one a soft-top, which were delivered to Middle Eastern customers at £100,000 each.

Ironically, in a car that at 4,360lb (1,962kg) weighs substantially more than the Jaguar XJ6/12 cars from which it derives most of its mechanical components, the De Ville is most commonly equipped with the Jaguar 4.2-litre straight-six engine. While the silky smooth 5.3-litre V12 would seem the logical choice in such a heavy car – and incidentally would take the car to beyond 130mph (209kph) despite aerodynamics like a brick wall – the restricted airflow through the tall, upright radiator means that in any hot climate, use of the V12 would be out of the question.

If weight may seem to be an impediment to all-out performance on paper, this is not borne out on the road and the De Ville can be made to move along quite briskly on the smaller engine. If it has any dynamic shortcomings, these centre around a power steering set-up that is far too light, though the problems are no worse than those of the Jaguar XJ saloons. The suspension is pure Jaguar. Springs and dampers are uprated all round, but in fact these parts are already available for the Daimler limousine, whose weight is not dissimilar to the Panther's.

These parts suspend a rectangular-section steel ladder chassis which is the backbone of the car and upon which the all-aluminium, hand-beaten coachwork finds its resting place. Only the doors are pressed steel and that is because they are Austin Maxi units. The front doors are unaltered, but the rear ones have to be reworked to suit the wheel arches of the De Ville. If you order

electrically operated windows, then the internal door skins are modified to take Jaguar electric window gear. On two-door versions, the doors come from the Jaguar XJC. In the saloon, all the door glass is Austin Maxi but front and rear windscreens are Panther and are laminated.

The aluminium panels are hand-beaten from flat sheet steel over steel and glass fibre formers. The wings, however, with their complex curves are made up from four or five sections welded together.

Aluminium will not rust away but it does oxidize on the surface and to protect the material, a special etching primer is used prior to hand-spraying 24 coats of two-pack Glasurit which is dried in a low-bake oven. Not even a Rolls-Royce can boast the luxury of so many coats!

Build time per car depends on the specification, but the last coupé took 4,000 hours. A saloon would be generally less than that, but Prince Sulaiman's car took 18 months.

The running boards along the side

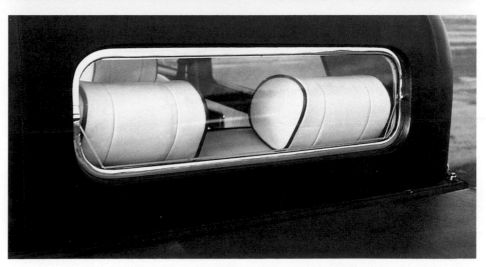

Above Whereas the Jaguar XK engine fits snugly, the V12 bulges out, necessitating conspicuous cowlings either side of the slender nose. The venerable twin-cam XK motor, especially mated to an automatic gearbox, hardly provides enough power, however, and its multi-cylindered stablemate provides much greater verve

Top right The modern headlamps are enclosed in larger cases more befitting the style of the Thirties.

Centre and bottom right Detailing on the Panther is excellent, a testimony to true craftsmanship. Chrome finning for the bonnet air extractors and piping for the headrests are just a few of the detail 'niceties'

of the car are immensely strong and would make the car very safe in the event of a side-impact accident, although the car has not been required to comply with any safety laws because of its very low build numbers. These running boards are made from laminated mahogany mounted on steel outriggers and covered with an aluminium skin to blend into the wings. They are then topped with a stainless steel scuff cover which you stand on when getting in and out of the car.

The luggage compartment at the rear on to which the spare tyre is mounted is rather an impractical shape for hard suitcases but is almost like a trunk itself. Its size can be specified and the rear chassis rails lengthened, if need be.

The radiator grille is made from brass and the 'mesh' itself is a woven pattern, just like a basket. The radiator cap is plain on later cars, but you can identify the earlier Panther Westwinds-built De Villes by the amethyst on their caps.

Should you nudge another car in the car park or if the car in front stops suddenly, your investment is protected by the telescopic bumper system with nylon inserts which disappear into tubes to absorb the impact.

Getting into the De Ville can be rather awkward: you have to work on the technique of opening the door, stepping on the running board and then ducking to clear the roof as you climb in. Once inside, you are cossetted in the Connolly hide seats which are based on Jaguar frames. In the traditional British idiom, polished wood cappings adorn the tops of the doors and form the instrument panel, which takes its full instrument display from the Jaguar XJ saloon. The huge,

four-spoke, leather-bound wheel is typical of period cars in its design but not its feel, which is contemporary and very comfortable in the hands. Vision out of the tiny rear window through the rear-view mirror is not helped by the optional rear head rests and you are thankful for the door-mounted, remotely adjustable mirrors. Rear leg room is generous but the narrow cabin allows only two passengers in comfort, three at a squeeze on the leather-covered bench.

On the road, the De Ville is not all that you would expect. Not much attention has been paid to engine- and road-derived noise; you can clearly hear the engine earning its keep under the long prow, while the ride on the 235/70HR15 Avon tyres does not approach the silky absorbence of the Jaguar's.

For all that, the Panther has character, stemming from its quirky mobile-gin-palace aesthetics (which in some ways border on the kitsch); its less-than-perfect road manners; and the effect it has on other road-users and bystanders. That is what the Panther De Ville will be remembered for in a hundred years' time.

Although not a true replica of the Bugatti Royale, the Panther De Ville is styled in the same vein. As with the Excalibur, the rear trunk is not an integral part of the design, while the running boards are again more for style

QUASAR
PEUGEOT

I n 1984 Peugeot, traditionally associated with rather staid passenger cars, shocked and thrilled the world by joining the high-performance hatchback league with its chic, nimble and very fast 205GTi. At almost the same time, all the existing models in its saloon range received fuel injection or turbocharging to make them

competitive with the crop of fast saloons in rival catalogues.

In the same year Peugeot's second milestone in the performance-car world was the twin-cam, 16-valve, turbocharged and four-wheel-drive 205 Turbo 16 which was to be built in limited numbers to contest the World Rally Championship for the marque. Winning it first time out in

1985 was no mean achievement, and has prevented Peugeots from ever being thought of again as mundane saloon cars for ageing drivers.

Even before the 205 Turbo 16 began to chalk up its rally successes, Peugeot engineers had devised other plans for the enticing mechanical package. They set about clothing it in

The Quasar is an attractively aggressive but elegant concept car with power and traction to back up its looks

Previous pages
Peugeot has for
many years relied on
Pininfarina for the
design of many of its
production cars, but
stunned the
motoring world
when it showed the
'in-house' Quasar.
The stylists have
been careful to
incorporate a
company identity
into the look: witness
the typical Peugeot
odd-angle
headlamps

Main picture The
Quasar's dashboard
is built around the
Clarion Car
Electronics System
(CCES) which gives
information not only
about the car's
functions but road
information and
even maps of your
planned route

Above Liquid-crystal
information is used
for the regular
gauges and the
heating and
ventilation system

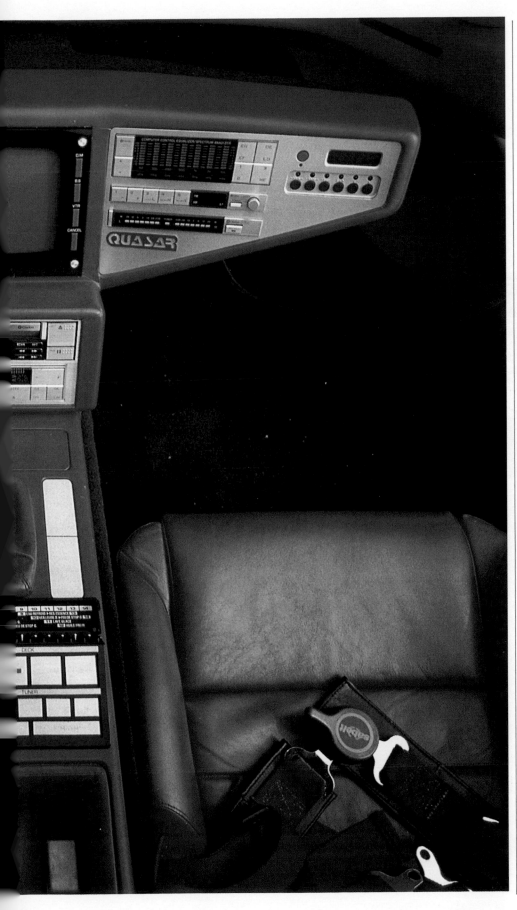

a sleek bodyshell housing state-of-the-art electronic gear, and it became their interpretation of the sports car of the future. The Quasar was designed in-house by Peugeot's own stylists at La Garenne and made its world debut on home ground at the 1985 Paris Motor Show.

Looking at the initial design sketches, it becomes clear that the Quasar was designed with deliberate science fiction overtones, an unrestricted brief and therefore no particular need to make concessions for possible production. Visually, many of the aspects of the car are sculptural, with a dramatically sloping nose incorporating the distinctive Peugeot corporate grille; slim, flush-fitting headlamps; a gigantic glass canopy swept by a single parallelogram wiper; massive side intake ducts; and an exposed engine with chrome-plated, 'French horn', megaphone twin exhaust system and massive air-to-air inter-cooler which sits transversely across the rear. The doors pivot forwards and up, giving the car the look of a massive insect that has come to rest on the ground.

The heart of the car is the 1,775cc, four-cylinder, twin-case, 16-valve engine with twin inter-cooled turbochargers. In its more basic form in the 205 Turbo 16 homologation special, this engine has a single Garrett AiResearch turbocharger boosting at 36psi. Coupled to an inter-cooler and water injection, this produces 430bhp at 7,500rpm. With a lowish 7:1 compression ratio and a big turbo, the turbo lag is marked when the engine is not spinning in its working range.

For even more power and quicker spin-up time, a twin turbo

installation using a pair of smaller units is preferable and this is precisely the route Peugeot has taken with the Quasar's engine. Output is boosted to around 600bhp which will give this compact and light car more than just dramatic performance.

To enable it to stay on the road with this sort of horsepower, the drivetrain of the Quasar had to be capable of putting the power down in all conditions and to this end an FF

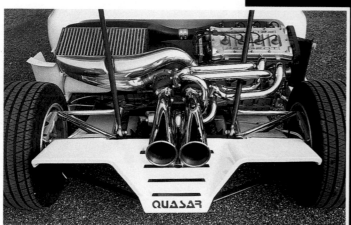

Above The turbo 16-valve engine, with its impressive, if overstyled, chrome-plated exhaust

Right The T16 Peugeot rally engine endows the Quasar with sensational performance

Developments four-wheel-drive system is employed with a 40:60 front-to-rear power-split ratio being applied via a centre differential. There are limited-slip differentials at each end and an anti-slip control system. A Formula-One-style suspension system is used with independent double wishbones, links and rocker arms at each corner with coil over damper struts. Each corner also wears a ventilated disc brake and a fat 255/50VR16 Michelin MXX tyre on an aerodynamically designed alloy wheel.

Inside the light and airy cockpit,

which is finished in dark blue and red leather, a phalanx of electronic gadgets confronts the driver. Directly ahead is a liquid crystal digital dashboard display with information on road and engine speed, fuel, average speed, distance, and service intervals, as well as ventilation. Conventional stalks are used on the steering column for lights, direction indicators and the horn.

The highlight of the interior, however, is the CCES (Clarion Car Electronics System), developed by Clarion, Japan's largest manufacturer of in-car entertainment equipment. While major car-makers are using solid-state electronics increasingly in their products, Clarion is heavily involved in the research and development of prototype maintenance, navigation and road-traffic information systems.

Although Clarion unveiled its second-generation C-AVCC (Car-Audio, Visual, Computer and Communication) system in a car of its own design at a press conference in Frankfurt in March 1986 and is well on the way to producing a third-generation system, the Peugeot Quasar was the first public showing of the C-AVCC system.

A large screen is incorporated into the centre console and this has selectable modes to offer control over the 14-point safety check, navigation, Teletel and audio systems. If, for instance, you select audio control, you are next presented with a choice between tape, tuner, compact disc or graphic equalizer.

The appropriate graphic display shows things like volume, treble, bass and track which you can see being altered as you touch the appropriate volume or selector controls.

In navigation mode, the CRT will display local maps and detailed street plans, while the Teletel gives advanced warning of road and traffic conditions ahead as broadcast from sub-stations. There is also a rear view mode to help make reversing considerably easier.

The Quasar is an attractively aggressive and yet elegant concept car with power and traction to back up its looks. And yet that is almost not enough in this quickly advancing electronics age. That the Japanese still lead the world in solid-state electronics is obvious; that the Quasar capitalizes on the latest Japanese developments and on the superior engineering and styling of Western manufacturers is yet another indication of the gains to be made from working to further east-west co-operation.

The Peugeot Quasar beside a streamlined 402 from the same stable. The 402, designed by Andrean, looked as modern in 1940 as the Quasar does now over 40 years later

959 GRUPPE B

PORSCHE

The world first learned all about both the Ferrari GTO (see pages 72-9) and the Porsche 959 homologation cars in 1983. By early 1986 all the Ferraris had been delivered to their delighted owners, but at Weissach, while all the 250 production 959s had been spoken for with hefty deposits from their would-be owners, it was expected that it could well be 1987 before the £100,000-plus machines went into production.

The issue is not one of Porsche's relative inefficiency. Far from it, for beyond the fact that both Ferrari GTO and Porsche 959 are homologation specials, they have

almost nothing in common. The Ferrari was by far the simpler car to produce, if only because all its advanced features were logical extensions of tried and tested technology honed to a finer edge. In configuration and construction it is a classical Ferrari, only better. The Porsche, on the other hand, breaks so much new ground in all respects from tyres to aerodynamics, that it has required an intensive and ongoing development programme which has included actual competitive rallying to prepare it for production. When ready, it should be the most capable sports car the world has ever seen.

The Type 959 has been under constant evolution since it was first unveiled at Frankfurt in September 1981. A shot in the arm for the 911 Series, provided by the new Chairman of Porsche, Peter W. Schutz, who had taken over the helm in January of that year, the car first appeared as a design study in the form of a four-wheel-drive 911 Turbo Cabriolet. The open-top configuration was subsequently incorporated into the 911 model line-up and the 959 development soon took a strong tangential direction all on its own, becoming ever more advanced.

By September 1983, the final form the car would take had been decided and it was time for the marketing department to start lining up customers and taking deposits. The following January, a 959 lookalike won the Paris-Dakar Rally, but in truth this car bore more 911 Carrera parts than 959 (apart from a simplified 4WD system).

The keys to the 959's technology are the four-wheel drive and suspension systems, both of which are state-of-the-art computer-controlled. One of the reasons why the details of the car's final specification are being kept quiet is that they are constantly changing. All the cars built so far have been of an experimental nature and therefore different from each other.

The four-wheel drive is a variable

The Porsche 959 has been under constant evolution since it was unveiled in 1981. When finished, it will be the most capable sports car ever seen

Left and above
Underneath the Porsche 959's curved body, the 911's line can still be detected. This car is much sleeker, however, and gets its stability from the overall shape of the body.
Previous pages The variable front-to-rear power balance can be used to set the 959 up into any cornering stance. A full-blooded power slide like this would be difficult to catch in the rear-wheel-drive 911

torque split system but with far, far greater sophistication than the simple viscous-couple systems used by Ford or VW. Those react to situations and are therefore always a little bit late. The Porsche system has a four-position manual override which lets the driver anticipate conditions ahead and engage the correct 'programme', which is then computer-controlled. These four programmes are for Dry, Wet, Snow and Traction, the last of which locks the drive solid for emergencies. In principle, the less traction on the road surface, the more equal the torque split. Within each of the four ranges, electronically controlled variations of the pressure applying the hydraulically operated multi-plate clutch, that passes torque from the rear to the front wheels, look after the rear to front power split. If the car is accelerated hard (this being 'read' from the selected gear and throttle opening), the pressure on the clutch decreases as weight is transferred from the front to the rear axle. At the same time, the computer

programme is taking into account any significant difference in the rotational speed between front and rear wheels, so that if the rear ones should start to spin, the clutch immediately increases its grip again to transfer torque back to the front wheels.

A seemingly minor, but in practice very significant detail is that the front wheels are very slightly larger in diameter than those at the rear. This has been achieved by making the 17-inch (43cm) diameter rims 1 inch (2.5cm) smaller at the front. With the front wheels thus revolving very marginally more slowly than the rear ones, under all normal conditions, they are thus forced to take a positive role in driving the car, and also promote a minimal slip in the coupling clutch. According to Porsche, the clutch is also used to influence the handling of the car as required and at high speed its grip is increased to impart more of the kind of understeer characteristic of front-wheel-drive vehicles when coping with fast bends (a stabilizing factor) while the clutch is freed as soon as the brakes are applied, leaving the standard ABS anti-lock braking system to work unhindered.

Electronics also govern the suspension control with respect to ride height and damping. A double wishbone suspension is used at each corner and there is a pair of gas-filled dampers for each wheel. One of these aluminium, lightweight units regulates ride height while the other acts as a normal damper. The driver

can choose from three settings – soft, normal and hard – but as soon as the car reaches speed, the dampers are switched on to the hard setting irrespective of the driver's choice. The ride height is also speed-governed, being at its lowest point 1 1/4 inches (30mm) lower, when the car exceeds 90mph (145kph). It can also be raised by another 1 1/4 inches (30mm) at low speeds to increase clearance on bumpy roads.

Another novelty is the 'thinking' wheel and tyre combination that has

been adopted because of the obvious safety questions raised by travel at 186mph (300kph). Dunlop Denloc safety tyres are thus standard footwear and these will prevent the 235/40VR17 and 255/40VR17 rubber moving laterally off the rim, should air pressure suddenly be lost. But if the unexpected happens, the driver is forewarned by an optical and audio alarm system. Sensors sit in the hollow part of the wheels and pick up possible tears in the casing. This is an extension of the system Porsche

has used in its Group C racers.

Right from the start the 959 was intended to be not only the fastest sports car in the world, but also the easiest to drive in city traffic. In order to obviate turbo lag, the engine development team, under Paul

The 959 is much wider than the 911 on which it is based, and all the panels flow into an integrated hole. The car's aerodynamics have been tried at over 200mph (322kph) at Le Mans where the car has run in its circuit-racing guise. In long-distance rallies, it has been virtually unbeatable

Hensler, used twin compound turbochargers which give a much faster response time than a single large unit. These two inter-cooled units feed air to a common plenum chamber on top of the engine where it then flows through a single throttle valve and into each combustion chamber via a six-branch intake manifold. This engine, which is similar in configuration to the 911's flat-six, is in fact partly water-cooled. The mixed cooling system, which uses water-cooled cylinder heads and the proven axial-fan cooling of the block, also provides a much more reliable heating system inside the car as a by-product. Four valves per cylinder are used in the heads of the 2850cc engine which develops 450bhp at 6,500rpm and 369lb ft of torque at 5,500rpm with an 8:1 compression ratio and electronic engine management. The supreme flexibility of the power unit is illustrated by the torque curve which describes over 300lb ft, nearly as much as the full torque of the 911 Turbo 3.3, being available from 2,200rpm right through to the 8,000rpm rev limit! In IMSA racing trim, the stripped competition version produces 650bhp.

With final production versions not as yet in the pipeline, Porsche is not really talking about performance figures, but it is speculated that the slippery new car with its Cd of 0.32 should be able to top 185mph (298kph) and break the 5-second mark on the 0–60mph (0–97kph) sprint.

The starting point of the 959's bodywork is an ordinary, galvanized steel 911 monocoque with altered suspension pickup points and a widened engine bay. Lighweight doors and engine cover are fabricated from aluminium, but the panels which actually give the 959 its distinctive appearance are formed from Aramid lightweight plastic bonded by the autoclave technique. Polyurethane front and rear panels protect the car from minor bumps.

'Form follows function' being a tenet of the 959's design, the car's functional beauty is derived from aerodynamic addenda that create a negative lift situation for stability at speed, and the air intakes on the four corners serve the oil and water radiators and the pair of air-to-air inter-coolers at the rear.

Inside, the 959 would be mostly familiar to a seasoned 911 driver and in that respect is dated. The appeal of the 911 has not waned in the face of more modern alternatives, however, and while the 959 could conceivably be described as having its roots in the original 356 concept, its spectacular 1–2–3 placing in the 1986 Paris-Dakar Rally has effectively silenced any critics.

Even on treacherous surfaces like packed snow, the all-wheel drive of the 959 ensures that it will accelerate rapidly. The extra grip afforded by 4WD and a sophisticated braking system make sure that the Porsche corners and stops just as well in those same conditions

PORSCHES 929, 939, 949 AND 969

RINSPEED

Every year in March, you can expect to see a new and spectacular offering from Rinspeed at the Geneva Motor Show. It was the 1981 Geneva Show in particular that put this Swiss firm on the map, for although it had been turning out modified Golfs and BMWs for several years, it is the

Rinspeed gullwing Golf with its Porsche 928 interior that visitors to the show that year will remember especially.

Frank Rinderknecht, a mechanical engineer and self-taught designer, is the creative brain behind the company and it was he who conceived that one-off Golf which was sold to a customer in the South of France. For the 1982 Geneva Show Rinderknecht presented a targa-top Golf with a fully electronic dashboard display and on-board computer. Continuing this line of Golf showcars, he had plans to build an even more outlandish project – an amphibious Golf – but shelved that idea in favour of a more commercially safe range of modified Porsches which would attract a steady flow of wealthy clients from around the world.

Browsing through a Porsche model range brochure, you won't come across the designation 939. This car came into being when

Previous pages The Rinspeed Turbo 939 is another 'clean' variation on the 911 Porsche; 928 Porsche-style lights are used

Above This show car has restrained NACA ducts on the rear flanks, but the style was changed for production models

Rinderknecht realized that there was a gap in the Porsche line-up for a cabriolet with the Turbo engine and decided to build such a car himself. He set about strengthening the car to take the extra power and at the same time incorporated a number of styling changes, including a 928-type flatnose with pop-up headlamps, a new bumper/spoiler unit with built-in driving lights, side skirts and a new rear section with Porsche 928 tail-lights. A pair of NACA ducts on top of the rear wings aid engine cooling. With an 882lb (397kg) weight advantage over the stock Turbo, the Rinspeed car claims to reach speeds of 170mph (274kph) and to complete the 0–60mph (0–97kph) sprint in 4.8 seconds. Rumour has it that Porsche

Top and bottom left The 928 influence is evident in the rear lights of the Rinspeed 939, too, while the full convertible body makes this one of the most desirable of Porsche-based cars. The 'whale tail' has been moved forwards to make the car look more compact

was so impressed with the result that it was that company which decided to go ahead and award the car the 939 model designation.

Rinspeed's production 939 cars differ slightly in appearance from the prototype seen at Geneva in 1983. The latest cars still use the same front section, with its huge intake for the oil-cooler and brake-cooling ducts,

but the NACA ducts have been removed from the tops of the rear wings to be replaced by a slatted intake on the leading edge of the rear arch, which in fact is a factory option on the Turbo which can be selected from the *Sonderwunch* ('Special Wish') catalogue.

Another innovation is a forward extension of the Turbo whale tail

spoiler which emphasizes the car's line and form. All the cars sit on 8 × 15-inch (20 × 38cm) and 12 × 15-inch (30 × 38cm) Gotti alloy wheels which are furnished with massive P7s of 205/50VR15 and 345/35VR15 section.

Interior trim can be anything your heart desires, but most of the Rinspeed cars leave the Zurich factory

Interior trim can be anything you desire, but most Rinspeed cars have leather-trimmed Recaro seats, dashboard and doors, with stereo, TV and even video

with leather-trimmed Recaro seats, dashboard and door panels and a full complement of component stereo and even TV and video sets. A typical Rinspeed aid to controlling and adjusting all this gear is to build some sort of remote control for the extensive sound system into the

Left What extra can be offered for the interior, apart from cramming every last spare inch with stereo and fitting the most comfortable electrically adjusted seats available? **Below and below right** Perhaps the standard instruments (below) can be substituted for colour-coded ones (below right), which were popular on Formula One race cars in the Fifties

steering-wheel boss!

Following on the heels of the 939 came the 929 based on the 928, and naturally enough the designation 949 was bestowed on the Rinspeed version of the 944. The factory beat Rinspeed to the model number 959, however, so the car displayed at the Geneva Show in 1985 became the 969.

If your first reaction is to think how much the 969 resembles the Ferrari Testarossa, it should be pointed out that the design was pretty much

determined in the summer of 1984 before the launch of the Italian car. While the 939 takes its inspiration from the 928, the 969 is more in the 944 idiom, with its bulging front wheel arches and 944 pop-up headlamps. An interesting detail is the small spoiler built into the leading edge of the nose. This sits about 2 inches (5cm) proud of the body but flush with the wings, and is angled to provide some downforce at speed. There is an aerofoil mounted on the trailing edge of the

roof and the squared-off rear incorporates a pair of air scoops on its top surface to supplement the cooling provided by the massive side intakes. The sheer width of these wheel arches has to be filled out by 225/50VR15 and 345/35VR15 P7s on 8½ × 15-inch (22 × 38cm) and 13 × 15-inch (33 × 38cm) Gotti wheels.

The bodywork can be fitted to a new or used 911 Turbo and although glass fibre is normally the material used by Rinspeed, the 969 style is also available in Kevlar.

Engine modifications can be undertaken to increase the stock 300bhp to 375bhp and the four-speed gearbox replaced with a close-ratio five-speed for even more dramatic acceleration.

The pearlescent white 969 showcar is finished in light grey leather and features Recaro Ideal C seats, with power-operated backrests and seat-heating. A Pioneer Centrate sound system was installed and this has a CD player, cassette deck, tuner and graphic equalizer, along with a sub-woofer speaker system. All this is driven by four 60-watt power amplifiers and has a remote control unit built into the four-spoke steering wheel.

Whatever you may have heard about Swiss neutrality, the people of that nation take their motoring pleasures seriously. It is not widely known that they have a private test track, complete with control tower and fondue-serving restaurant, where you can test high-performance cars to your heart's content. Advanced driving courses are conducted here and this is where Rinspeed obtains some of its performance data and assesses the handling of its cars.

Rinspeed is the Swiss agent for AMG Mercedes conversions and still carries a catalogue full of body-styling parts for VW and BMW cars. But most of these are brought in from West Germany and the company acts merely as distributor in Switzerland. Frank Rinderknecht's pride and joy remains his exclusive line of Porsche conversions – his brainchild and company showcase.

The Rinspeed 969 takes the Porsche Turbo concept one stage further. A full upswept tail obviates the need for a bolt-on wing and thus produces less aerodynamic drag for its improved stability. Power is up by 25 per cent

SAAB

EV-1

SAAB

It wasn't so long ago that the sports car breed was pronounced almost dead. The demise of the Triumph TRs, MGs and others left enthusiasts with just a handful of prestigious and expensive exotics and an even smaller group of ageing survivors headed by the Fiat X1/9. Recent months, however, have witnessed a profound alteration to this gloomy picture and sports cars are very much back in vogue. Significantly, some of the companies rushing in to fill the void have been those major manufacturers, like Toyota and Pontiac, who formerly shunned such 'irrelevancies'.

The Swedish firm Saab, which has not been associated with sports cars since its ill-fated Sonnet over a decade ago, has been in the forefront of the high-performance saloon car market in recent years since the introduction of its 99 Turbo in 1976 and the 16-valve 900 Turbo in 1984. Certainly, the emphasis on practical design with a high-technology base has been Saab's watchword right from the start and is a logical carry-over from the firm's mainstay business of making aircraft. The dramatic styling and performance of the EV–1, which incidentally is a fully working prototype, is its answer to the question of what a sports car of the near future should be.

Unveiled at the Los Angeles Auto Expo in May 1985, the EV–1 'gives the opportunity to employ the materials and technical features of tomorrow', according to Saab. While it denies that the car is the forerunner of a future production design, it is not hard to see that under the skin, it has made full use of the Saab 'parts bin' and therefore could be brought to fruition rather more easily than many other show cars. Though utilizing uprated dampers, ventilated front disc brakes, wider tyres and increased front and rear track, the suspension is that of the Saab 900 Turbo 16S. Even more significant must be the use of the floorpan and chassis of the three-door 900 Turbo for this 2 + 2 coupé. And the engine? A further development of the 2.0-litre turbocharged 16-valve unit.

Further study of the great attention to detail that has been lavished upon the EV–1 makes it plain that this front-wheel-drive 2 + 2 could be more than simply an exotic show car. Styled by Bjorn Envall and his fellow staff at the Saab Design Centre, the emphasis upon 'optimum road behaviour' and practicality for 'four

adults and a vast amout of luggage', rather than outright glamour or a new Cd record figure, is an indication of the possible motives behind the car. The body is of modular design and the lines and functional features can be modified without involving any major changes to the car as a whole. This means that modifications for production to comply with legislation or tooling requirements as well as developing changes during the car's life, if it ever were to be produced, could be achieved with minimum expense.

The wedge-shaped, steel-bodied car with its smoothly contoured rear has no obvious aerodynamic additions apart from an integrated rear spoiler, but is designed to minimize lift and ensure good stability at high speeds. A distinctive feature is the all-glass upper section with targa top, a roof panel that can be lifted out. The rear window and boot lid have been integrated – not an unusual feature in Saab's design book. The flush-designed alloy wheels contribute to a clean aerodynamic profile but have concealed slots which draw in air to aid brake-cooling.

To enhance the homogenous look of the car, the EV–1 uses intergrated front and rear bumpers of aramide-fibre reinforced plastic. These can absorb impact elastically, in contrast to some designs which require separate bumpers to absorb and dissipate energy from impact. Another bonus with this material is its

extremely light weight. The front and rear shields weigh only 2.6lb (1.2kg) and 2.2lb (1kg) respectively and the lights can be integrated into the shields. Demonstrating once again the diversity of the Saab organization, these materials came from Saab Composite AB, a subsidiary of the parent company which develops composite materials for aerospace and other applications.

The Swedish have always been leaders in passive safety in cars and all production Saabs carry steel side-impact protection bars in their doors. In current terms of weight and therefore fuel efficiency, this is not an ideal material to use and Saab have incorporated a new composite material of reinforced glass fibre with a layer of carbon fibres into the doors of the EV–1. This new composite conforms to the strictest American side-impact protection standards and yet is only half the weight of a steel member of similar strength.

The lighter and more aerodynamic bodyshell of the EV–1 would in itself have contributed to a superior performance envelope for the Saab 900 Turbo 16-valve, but Saab further modified the EV–1's engine, with development work once again having possible consequences for standard production cars. Engine output has been boosted by increasing the sizes of the intake and exhaust systems, thus allowing higher rates of gas flow. Bosch LH-Jetronic fuel injection is used in combination with an inter cooled Garrett 1098 turbocharger and Saab's patented Automatic Performance Control (APC) system which allows the engine to adapt to varying grades of fuel. To enable the boost pressure to be raised to 15.6 psi, the compression ratio was reduced from

The EV-1 slips through the air smoothly, courtesy of a 0.32 drag coefficient. The nose of the car is similar to the company's production saloons

9:1 to 7.2:1 and the engine incorporates forged pistons and reinforced connecting rods. The result of this is a dramatic lift in power from 185bhp of the standard production 16-valve engine to 285bhp at 6,500rpm but perhaps more impressive is the maximum torque of 246lb ft at a moderate 3,500rpm. Despite not having a

dramatically low Cd as part of its design brief, the EV–1 easily achieves a Cd of 0.32 which, when multiplied by its small frontal area of 2 square yards (1.72m²), gives the low CdA value of 0.55. A top speed of 186mph (300kph) can thus be achieved and through the gears the EV–1 passes 60mph (97kph) in 5.4 seconds, 120mph (193kph) in 18.5 seconds

and the standing quarter mile (0.4km) in 13.9 seconds.

Beyond being merely a styling, packaging and engineering showcase, the Saab EV–1 also incorporates some very radical electronic advances. Taking into account the extraordinarily large expanse of glazing, there normally would be massive solar gain and

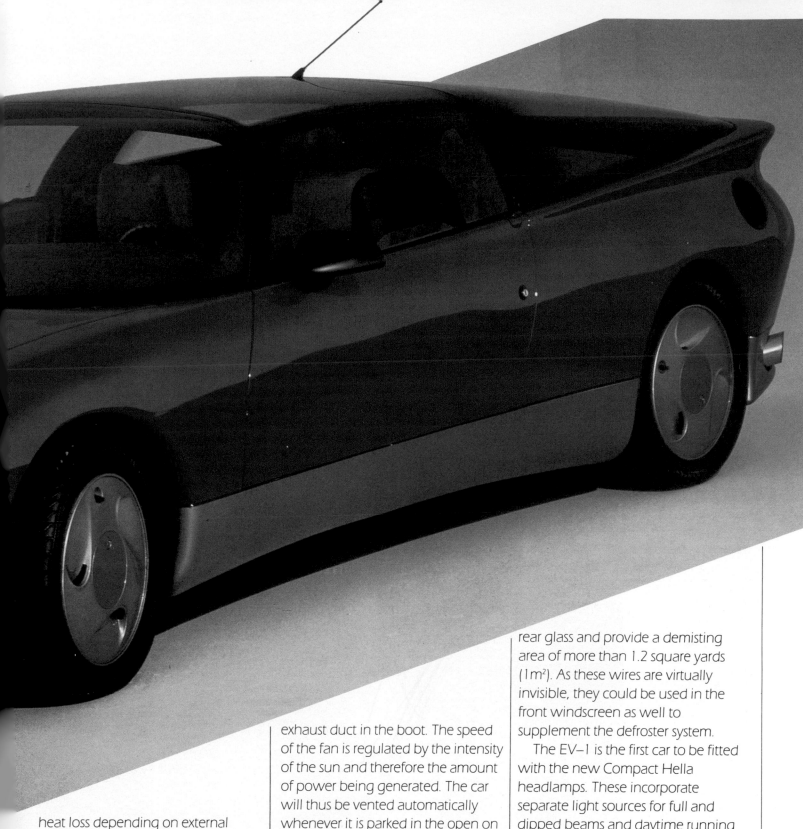

heat loss depending on external conditions, despite the fact that the windows are all heat-reflecting. While the basic climate control of the EV–1 is straight out of the Saab 900 along with its air-conditioning, the ventilation system is quite novel and has been patented by Saab. The removable glass targa top incorporates 66 solar cells connected in series which power an electric motor-driven fan mounted in the air

exhaust duct in the boot. The speed of the fan is regulated by the intensity of the sun and therefore the amount of power being generated. The car will thus be vented automatically whenever it is parked in the open on a sunny day. With less of a thermal load to cope with, the air-conditioning can thus reach preset temperature levels much faster once the car is started.

High-impact laminated glass is used for the front and rear windows and toughened glass for the rest. Hardly visible tungsten wires of 0.6 thou (0.015mm) diameter are built into the laminate sandwich of the

rear glass and provide a demisting area of more than 1.2 square yards (1m²). As these wires are virtually invisible, they could be used in the front windscreen as well to supplement the defroster system.

The EV–1 is the first car to be fitted with the new Compact Hella headlamps. These incorporate separate light sources for full and dipped beams and daytime running lights. Complementing the low and sloping front of the EV–1, the new lights have a higher intensity than current halogen designs and, being divided into separate parts, allow all available lights to be switched on at the same time.

Saab has always followed a consistent line in the design of its car instrumentation and this has been developed from experience in aircraft production and knowledge gained about pilots' reactions to various types of information. This information must always be clearly presented and not obscured by 'information noise' produced by less important details and signals. Following the 'Black Panel' principle, only relevant information is presented and is displayed in analogue form. For the EV–1, this philosophy has been further developed in conjunction with VDO, a specialist instrument company. The speedometer, no longer carrying a trip meter or mileometer, is fitted right in front of the driver and during night driving a unique lighting system throws light only on to the speed range in which the car is travelling. The instrument lighting can be switched on or off as required by manual control and is activated automatically if a warning system should come into operation.

The seats in the EV–1 are half the weight of conventional units as their chassis and backrest frame are made of injection-moulded plastic. All four seats are electrically adjustable backwards and forwards and for height. Additionally, the seat angle and side ridges of the front seat are adjustable for perfect comfort. All the seats are electrically heated with thermostatic control. Seat covering is leather while the cushions and lower backrests of the front seats are suede to stop occupants sliding around in hard cornering.

The 900 Turbo EV–1 has given Saab the opportunity to employ tomorrow's materials and technology in an advanced rolling test-bed. It is feasible and practical projects like this which must surely point the way to the next generation of production cars.

Far right The EV-1's interior is again very much like the production cars from the same stable with similar instruments and switchgear. That too points to production feasibility

Right The solar panels in the glass roof of the Saab power the car's ventilation system which works most of the daylight hours to cope with the heat build-up due to the glass roof

SBARR

GOLF AND GULLWING
SBARRO

Works of art do not come cheaply, whatever category they fall into, and the prices that Franco Sbarro will quote for the automotive works of art that roll out of his Swiss-based factory, ACA (Atelier d'Etudes de Construction Automobiles) most definitely put them in the wealthy collectors' class.

A Sbarro replica Ford GT40 will cost you about £55,000, with a Lola T70 at £70,000. If you are into the Thirties classics, then the Sbarro Mercedes 540K Special Roadster is

£80,000 and the Bugatti Royale only £7,000 more. If your tastes are more modest, then Sbarro's six-cylinder, BMW-engined BMW 328 replica must be a snip at a mere £18,000! It's also much faster than the original!

The choice extends beyond replicars, though, to the vehicles that have stamped Sbarro as one of the most talented and innovative constructors of unusual, luxury, high-performance cars in the world. Where many of the famous names in styling, like Pininfarina and Giugiaro, work hand in hand with major manufacturers to bring a design to running prototype form, ACA has the capability and in-house expertise to tackle all the mechanical design and fabrication work itself and has often been asked to produce one-off vehicles for major manufacturers because no other company could do the job for a comparable price.

For Franco Sbarro, born in 1939, the story began near Lecce, a town in the far south of Italy. The son of a farmer, he grew up with machinery around him and in his youth amused himself by assembling strange contraptions propelled by motor-cycle engines. His mechanical aptitude eventually took him across the Swiss border to Neuchâtel where he worked as a mechanic. Two years later, he bought a small agency handling products for Borgward, a car manufacturer based in the West German city of Bremen, and this ran for a while before joining a BMW dealer as workshop manager. It was only when he went to work for Georges Filipinetti at Château de Grandson that his aptitude for car-building came to the fore. As chief mechanic of the famous Scuderia Filipinetti racing team, Sbarro not only took care of the racing cars but

To wind up the cars you have just blown off at the lights, a hydraulic system enables the body of the car to be raised

also had the opportunity to oversee the restoration of the odd AC Cobra, Ferrari P3 and Ford GT40. He also built his first one-off sports car down in the cellars of the castle and christened it the Filipinetti Coupé. This car was based on a VW Karmann Ghia floorpan and had a 1,200cc engine. Two years later, the Coupé Filipinetti II appeared with a 1,600cc engine. At this point Sbarro decided it was time to leave.

April 1968 found Sbarro with workshop facilities in a converted cigarette factory. His first car was called the Dominique III and was a low-slung sports car with a large spoiler on the back. This was not a resounding success; only one was made and thankfully sold. After that, Sbarro exploited a new market by converting racing GT40s to road-going trim and completed four of these conversions before building seven from scratch, one of which was based on De Tomaso Pantera running gear. ACA extended the appeal of its racing replicar range with the Lola T70 of which 13 eventually were made. Most of these used Chevrolet V8 power, apart from the odd one with a Ferrari V12 or a Porsche Turbo motor. There is a story surrounding the Lola T70, which also demonstrates Sbarro's professionalism. It goes like this: a rich

Whether he is converting a standard Mercedes into a dramatic gullwing or building the ultimate 'Q-car' from scratch, Franco Sbarro never fails to create a work of art

Arab once walked into Sbarro's office, took a fancy to the Lola T70 he was building for a customer and offered a large sum of money for the car on the spot. When told that the car was already spoken for, the Arab increased the size of his bank roll. Sbarro, however, has integrity so he told the gentleman that the waiting list was still six months and that if he would like to order one, he could

even give him a precise delivery date. Exit Arab, *minus* T70.

Sbarro has nevertheless done a lot of business with Middle Eastern customers, including building the TAG (Techniques d'Avant-Garde) for Akram Ojjeh, an oil billionaire who wanted a mobile armoured conference room. The Sbarro Windhawk was built for King Khalid of Saudi Arabia to go hawking in and this even has a hydraulic lift to raise the seats 30 inches (76cm) above roof level! Long excursions are made possible by a 92-gallon (418-litre) petrol tank and a 40-gallon (182-litre) fresh water tank.

Sbarro has also outdone the major

Below Even Franco Sbarro has produced designs on the Mercedes-Benz coupé base. For many customers, money is no object and a king's ransom can be spent on body modifications alone. Extensive body strengthening, cutting and shutting has been carried out to produce this Gullwing

Inset Sbarro is keen to stylize the finished vehicle and uses slats on much of his work to produce a different look. The ribbed appearance of the standard Mercedes rear lights has been continued here into the adjoining panels, while a full-width grille has been incorporated

Above The owner of this Gullwing Mercedes has ordered 'go' as well as 'show' and has specified twin turbochargers for the V8 5-litre engine. Such modification will raise the car's top speed from a little over 135mph (217kph) to more than 170mph (274kph)

manufacturers by providing the world with a pair of the ultimate hot-hatchbacks in the form of the Super Twelve which comes complete with two six-cylinder 1,300cc Kawasaki motor-cycle engines in the back, each rated at 130bhp. This gives the glass fibre town car a 7.2lb (3.3kg) per horsepower power to weight ratio which enables the little chain-driven car to claw its way to 100mph (161kph) in under 8 seconds.

Less obvious is the rather standard-looking black Golf GTi which when

prodded will leave a Porsche Turbo in its wake. Where you would normally find the back seat in a Golf, there now sits a 345bhp Porsche Turbo engine and, like the rear-engined Porsche, this Golf has its fuel-tank in the front of the car. With two people on board, the car has a 50/50 weight distribution and has been clocked at 165mph (266kph). As a wind-up to the cars you have just blown off at the lights, a hydraulic system enables the body of the car to be raised, even on the move,

although this was devised to make maintenance easy.

For about £62,000, Sbarro will operate on a Mercedes 500SEC to produce what he has called the Mercedes 500 Portes Papillon Gullwing (butterfly gullwing doors). To strengthen the structure, he welds the bottom of the doors to the car, having dissected them from the rubbing stripline down, and cuts the tops into the roof. The wheel arches are enlarged to cover the wider wheels and a ribbed theme is carried round the car below the waistline. Perhaps the most dramatic view of the car is from the front, where the ribbed grille hides the lights when they are off. A rear spoiler finishes the tail in a kink.

Whether he is converting a standard Mercedes into a designer model for a specific customer, or building from scratch a 'Q-car' *par excellence*, Franco Sbarro always demonstrates that he has one of the most fertile minds in the world of dream cars.

Above Looking at the world through rose-tinted spectacles: the plush interior of the Gullwing, with acres of napp leather and walnut veneer and an unusual colour tint for the windscreen. Opulence and individuality go hand-in-hand on all Sbarro cars

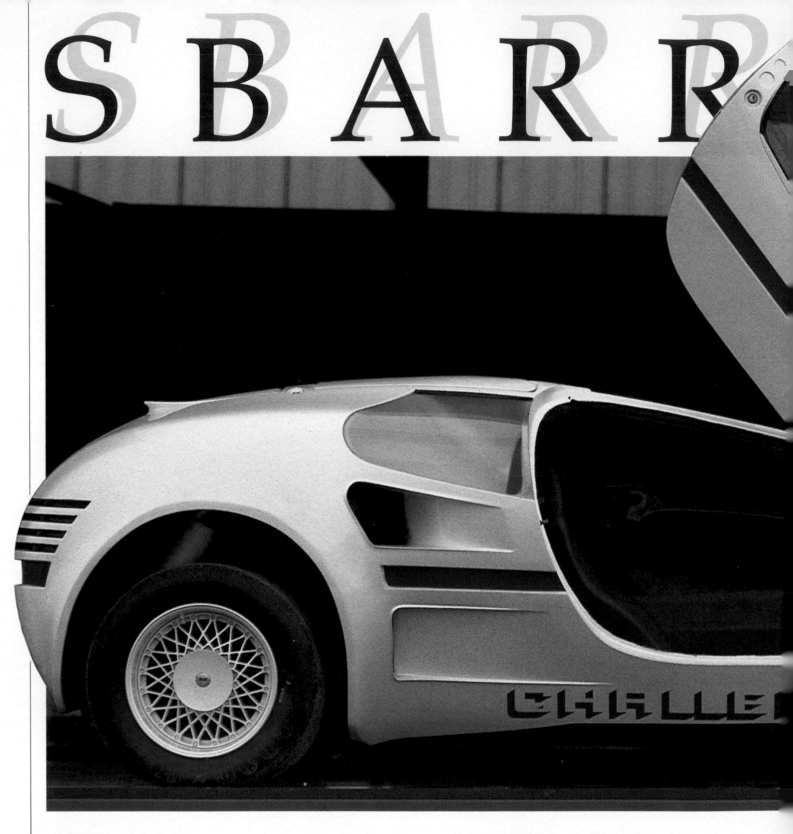

CHALLENGE
SBARRO

As for all his Swiss car-making compatriots, Geneva is the star show of the year for Franco Sbarro and so his working year usually begins a good nine months before the crowds gather in March.

Working to such a schedule, the running chassis of a new project is usually ready by September, the body a month later and some

semblance of the complete car will be ready by the time the staff depart to enjoy their Christmas dinner. It was in this way that the Challenge evolved in time for its 1985 Geneva debut.

This radical-looking sports car began life as a scale model and was crafted for Sbarro by a local toy designer! In concept, it is a very pure teardrop design, with a roofline sweeping up from a shovel nose and curving down over the back around a pivot point that is the huge rear-wheel centreline. On the model the doors were angular in their corners and the windows followed the roofline upwards after first having followed the angle of the doors down. Neat little cut-outs behind the trailing edges of the doors formed the fingerspaces for the hidden door catches. The huge discs on the wheels matched the curves of the body, as did the rear lights on the rounded rump of the vehicle.

With a dramatic model like this, Sbarro very quickly found an investor willing to pour the rumoured £100,000 for the prototype into his lap and the deal was sweetened by the promise of a percentage of the price of every subsequent car sold

In typical Sbarro fashion, the performance of the Challenge equals its visual beauty — the car reaches a Ferrari Boxer-eating 186mph (300kph)

going back into the investor's kitty.

In typical Sbarro fashion, the performance of the car had to equal its visual beauty, so it came as no surprise to the crowds at Geneva that the Challenge, as the car was named, wound up with a twin-turbocharged Mercedes 5-litre V8 engine tucked away amidships. The pair of Japanese-made IHI turbochargers squeeze 350bhp out of the big V8 and this is usable in all weathers, thanks to a four-wheel-drive American Motors transmission from a Cherokee Jeep, complete with high and low ratios and automatic transmission. In low ratio, the Challenge can thus zoom away from rest with almost ridiculous acceleration and then move into its high ratios on the motorway where the turbos and the good aerodynamics will push the car up to a Ferrari Boxer-eating 186mph (300kph).

Four months from the beginning

Previous pages With a clean sheet of paper, Sbarro's mind can run into overdrive to create a whole new look
Below The Challenge is a mid-engined bolide with performance to match its looks
Right The interior is strangely archaic and looks like a development hack, but high-tech still abounds
Far right The video window in the rear gives the driver a view behind to help in tight spaces

of the project, the basic monocoque tub was complete, with the engine, transmission and suspension installed and a cage of steel tubing joining it all together. Running tests began on a nearby unopened stretch of autoroute and with all the mechanicals sorted out, intensive work began to scale up the model around the running gear.

The general shape of the body was built up with thin steel rod, one bar of which was placed every 8 inches (20cm) along the length of the body following the proposed cross section at that point. Before the glass fibre shell was draped over the car, it looked rather like a computer-aided-design skeleton drawing. From there, it was down to a lot of filler and rubbing down to arrive at the final shape from which the moulds would be taken. These were done in four parts: the two sides, the bonnet and the engine cover. The final bodyshell was ready just before Christmas 1984.

The real world of car-building sometimes does not even come close to the concept on paper or to the model car. This is because of the constraints placed upon the real thing by the size and shape of the off-the-shelf mechanical components and by considerations of space for occupants and luggage, as well as by legislation, although that is less of a problem in a vehicle that is not being built for mass production.

In the case of the Challenge, the engineering compromises have meant that much of the dramatically pure teardrop concept of the model has been lost and the car has ended up more of a wedge, lacking the continuous curves. The wheels don't

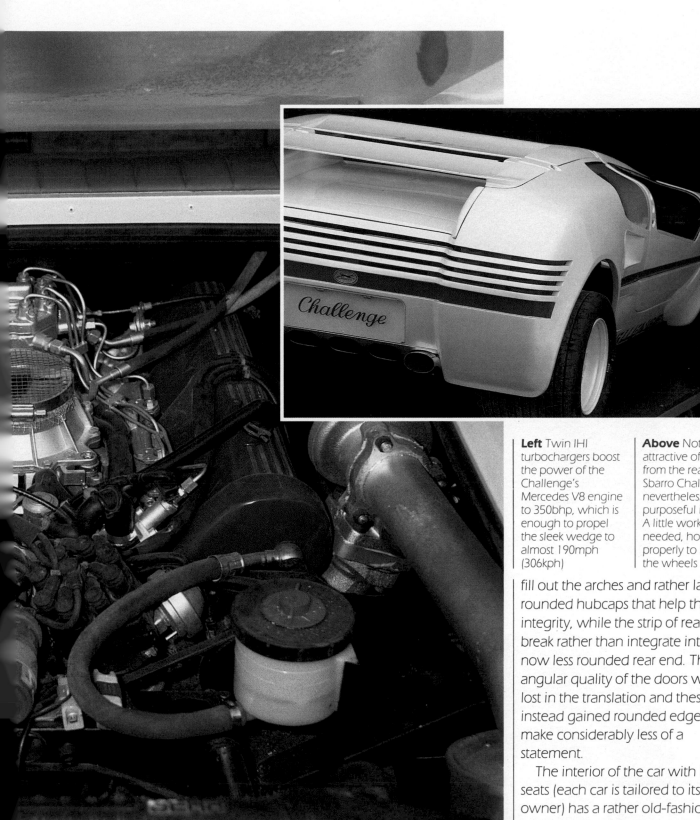

Left Twin IHI turbochargers boost the power of the Challenge's Mercedes V8 engine to 350bhp, which is enough to propel the sleek wedge to almost 190mph (306kph)

Above Not the most attractive of cars from the rear, the Sbarro Challenge is nevertheless purposeful in its line. A little work is needed, however, properly to integrate the wheels

fill out the arches and rather lack the rounded hubcaps that help the visual integrity, while the strip of rear lights break rather than integrate into the now less rounded rear end. The bold angular quality of the doors was also lost in the translation and these have instead gained rounded edges that make considerably less of a statement.

The interior of the car with its fixed seats (each car is tailored to its owner) has a rather old-fashioned dash with lots of mixed shapes in the instruments and controls, and a gigantic centre console for the transmission which cuts the interior in half. The door trims, in opposition

Franco Sbarro has thrown the traditional sports-car look out of the window for the Challenge, and his design is as sleek a wedge as can be imagined

to all that, look futuristic and moulded. Certainly the right names are there – seats by Recaro, stereo by Clarion, CD player by Pioneer, trim by Connolly and steering wheel by Nardi – but the final effect is less than homogenous.

Mechanically, however, the car

was a success, with the twin-turbo V8, adjustable ride height, twin rear spoilers that rise into the airstream as you increase speed and tilt to act as air-brakes when you want to stop, the gullwing doors, rear-view camera and the all-important Cd of 0.26 which was confirmed in Citroën's wind tunnel.

Four people demonstrated their delight with the finished car, and were more than ready to put down their £60,000 for a copy of the Challenge. Perhaps at the end of the day, exclusivity does tower above just about everything else.

PORSCHE 928S

STROSEK

Perhaps the last place you expect to see a lowered, widened and bespoilered supercar is in a quiet little German village in the middle of nowhere. But Utting, in beautiful rural Ammersee, south of Munich, plays hometown to Vittorio Strosek and, as a traditional village that has hardly changed in many years, makes an incongruous backdrop to the ultra-modern

K

Porsches that Strosek prepares for his customers at a nearby farmhouse. It is here that Strosek takes delivery of £30,000 sports cars – at least that is what the Porsche 928s cost when they arrive, for it is so very easy for the customer to run up a further bill for £10,000 on body, suspension, wheel-tyre and engine modifications and leave with a full-house twin-supercharged Version 3, the most visually aggressive 928S around.

But Strosek's claim to fame is not based entirely on his own line of conversions for the 928S and the recently added 944. A talented designer from the School of Automobile Design in Wuppertal, he spent a lucrative apprenticeship under the renowned Luigi Colani before setting up a design studio of his own. Early commercial design work was in fact on Porsche cars and Strosek designed a new front end for a VW Porsche 914. He also worked on the Eiffelland-March project in Formula-One racing but sadly this never reached fruition because of financial difficulties. In the late Seventies, he was extremely active in the aftermarket industry and in 1978 styled the famous EVEX flatnose Porsche 911 which is still on sale unchanged today.

While others use the 928 look for the 911, Vittorio Strosek starts with a 928 and changes its image completely

In 1981 Strosek made the decision to move from his home town of Düsseldorf in northern Germany to the more prosperous south-east, closer to the three manufacturers BMW, Mercedes and Porsche. Once in Bavaria, Strosek chose a rustic setting, which he says gives him the quiet inspiration he needs for creative design.

One of his first contacts, Willy Koenig, turned out to be his best customer. The meeting of these two car-lovers turned out to be a meeting of like minds too, and resulted in the Koenig Ferrari 512BB styling and all subsequent Koenig cars (see pages 99-113). Following this fruitful liaison, Strosek forged ahead with his own range of styling parts for the Porsche 928S. The reason for choosing the 928S over any of the other models in the Porsche range was a simple yet sound business decision to enter the market with a product for which there was little or no competition, a prolific number of 911 and 924 bits being already on offer.

Some aftermarket manufacturers choose to produce different kits for a particular car or only complete cars. Strosek, on the other hand, has devised a modular system known as Versions 1, 2 and 3, each a complete

The Strosek 928 looks
purposeful at speed,
and its deep spoiler
and carefully
integrated rear
wings ensure
stability

Above Use has been made of fluting ahead of the rear wheels, which Pininfarina is now incorporating into all new Ferrari designs. As well as strengthening the 928 identity with his bodywork, Strosek also manages to make his cars more efficient aerodynamically

model in its own right but capable of being added to, building up to the definitive Version 3. In this way, Strosek takes a single concept which can be elaborated upon according to the customer's taste and pocket.

The penny-pinching Version 1 radically alters the nose treatment of the 928 by replacing the deformable factory nose-cone with a new PU-RIM section and integral front spoiler. There is also an option for four powerful halogen lights to replace the frog-eye, pop-up lights of the original. Larger inlets in the new nose provide better brake- and engine-cooling. Aerodynamically, this sleeker snout improves penetration and reduces lift by 30 per cent. Downforce is increased by 150 per cent at the rear by a wing which has become something of a trademark

on all the Strosek-designed Koenig cars. Visually tied in by laminated side skirts and finished off with a rear skirt, the complete package reduces the drag coefficient of the bulbous Porsche from a rather drastic 0.39 to a more acceptable 0.37 while providing much more stable cornering and straight-line stability in cross-winds. The standard large, drag-inducing door mirrors are also replaced by aerodynamically designed units with either manual or electrical adjustment.

While the Version 1 looks visually complete with the standard wheels and tyres, you can also invest in a Strosek sport suspension kit which takes an inch (2.5cm) off ride height with tauter, shortened springs, uprated dampers and three-piece BBS alloy wheels of 8- and 9-inch

Above The bulbous wheel arches start from the door panels before they flow over the gumball rear tyres on their BBS three-piece alloy wheels

(20 and 23cm) width mounted with 245/45VR16 Pirelli P7 tyres.

If you take the Version 1 as being very much a 'bolt-on' replacement job apart from the laminated side skirts, then the Version 2 is where the skill of the bodyshop technicians really counts, with the fitting of wider flares at the rear to cover the 265/50VR16 tyres on 10-inch (25cm) rims that complement the 8-inch (20cm) wide fronts. The 6¾ inch (17cm) wider bodywork is typically Strosek, with elegant curves blending into the rounded bodywork and neat splits at the door shut-lines. The Strosek sport suspension is mandatory at this level to provide free movement of the large wheels on full spring deflection. When this car appears in your rear-view mirror, you can spot the difference between the

For the man who lives in a street full of Porsches, the Strosek full-house 928S Version 3 makes him without doubt the toughest kid on the block

Version 1 and 2 by the large air-box on the bonnet and the NACA ducts on its leading edge. Together, these provide 40 per cent more air flow and ease thermal build-up problems while driving in traffic.

The ultimate visual treat for a Strosek Porsche customer is the Version 3, which looks even more homogenous with its wider front flares covering 9-inch (23cm) wide front rims. At the rear, a spoiler on the trailing edge of the roof streams air more efficiently towards the wing and also improves extraction of internal air from the cabin vents without causing rearward blind spots. The plain, colour-coded hub-caps complete the aerodynamic look of the Version 3 and improve airflow to the brakes. Under the very strict German TUV regulations, no aftermarket aerodynamic addition should detract from stability or reduce the effectiveness of the brakes. Strosek's conversion parts enhance active safety by making the car more stable and improve braking efficiency by admitting more cooling air than in the standard car.

Having gone to the trouble of dressing up his car, it would be most embarrassing for the proud owner to be beaten away from the lights by a standard 928S. In fact, the body additions, in cleaning up the Cd, actually improve fuel consumption by 10 per cent and raise top speed by 7mph (11kph), but to improve acceleration at all speeds, Strosek turns the engine over to the famous German racing engine preparation firm, Probst & Mentel, who 'blueprint' it and add fairly mild camshafts with modified cylinder heads to bring power up by 40bhp to 350bhp. This is a fairly modest power increase (only 13 per cent), but the emphasis is on long-term

reliability and smoothness. So far there have been four customers who simply couldn't be content with a mere 350bhp and Strosek turned their engines over to a Swiss firm who bolted a pair of American MPD superchargers on to the engine, which then produced 400bhp with a modest 11psi boost.

A factory Porsche 928S can come very luxuriously appointed in leather with an eight-speaker hi-fi system, but for the very well-heeled customer, the trimmers at Strosek's factory are always ready to re-upholster cars to order and fit all sorts of electronic gadgets, from on-board computers to TV sets. At the end of the day, it is simply a question of money, but for the man who lives in a street full of Porsches, the Strosek 928S Version 3 makes him without doubt the toughest kid on the block.

Headlamps set into the nose, a full-width chin spoiler, NACA ducts on the bonnet, and wide and low aggressive stance separate the Strosek car from the standard item. Plain wheel covers can be specified which are more efficient aerodynamically than the spoked alloy items, and they blend into the design more comfortably, too

STYLING

MERCEDES-BENZ MARBELLA, ARROW, ROYALE AND ST TROPEZ

STYLING GARAGE

It is ironic that the Arab States, responsible for the two oil crises that the world has seen in the past 15 years, are themselves the most conspicuous consumers of ostentatious and fuel-hungry luxury cars.

The tremendous wealth generated by oil money created a whole new

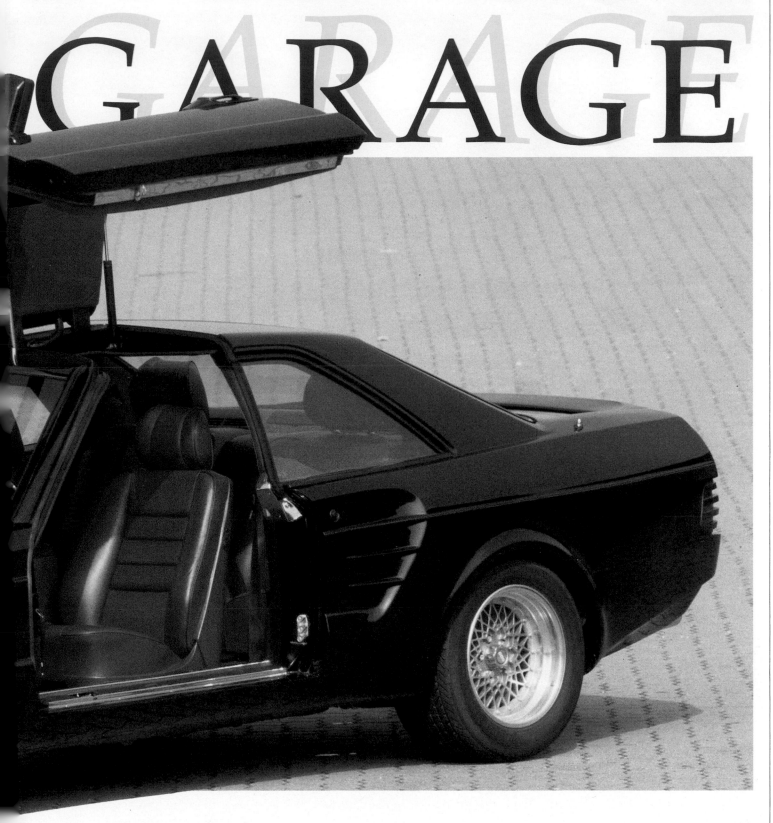

industry almost overnight, an extension of the bespoke coachbuilding trade that has been with us since the early days of the motor car. Previously, a handful of established names, such as Hooper and Tickford, stood for what was by no means a prominent part of the motor industry. And then, in the Seventies, the sudden demand for mobile symbols of one-upmanship

saw a mass of companies springing up all over Europe to cash in on this sudden windfall. Today, in Germany alone, there are 21 companies converting Mercedes cars to order.

Founded in 1979, Styling Garage (SGS) was rather a late starter in the game, but soon shot to prominence through a series of radical, sometimes bizarre-looking devices built for Arab customers with a taste for the

unusual. The story of Styling Garage is not exactly straightforward, however, and there was certainly an element of fate involved in its founding. The present proprietor, Chris Hahn, a marine engineer by profession, with a great interest in racing motor cycles and off-roading in four-wheel-drive vehicles, drove one day on to the forecourt of a small company called Styling Garage

which sold American Jeeps and various aftermarket accessories for them. In West Germany, a motor workshop cannot be licensed unless it is run by a qualified engineer and Styling Garage did not have an engineer in residence. When the proprietor at that time, Ralph Engel, found out that Chris Hahn was an engineer, he offered him a job on the spot and within a year Hahn became an equal partner in the business. Another year passed during which time Chris produced several converted luxury cars for customers. 'There is a limit to what you can do to cheaper cars because of what their owners can afford', he says, 'so it was obvious right from the start that we would only work with Mercedes cars.'

At the end of 1982 Chris bought

out his partner and moved to larger premises where he not only produces his elaborate conversions of new cars, but also undertakes the restoration of Mercedes-Benz 600 limousines and 300SL Gullwings. Styling Garage, with its renowned coachbuilding skills, also does contract work, such as producing convertible VW Polos and BMWs, for local dealers.

The Arab market on which the fortunes of Styling Garage and so many other firms were built has shrunk dramatically since 1983. Now making a more concerted effort to market in Europe, the company has undergone a radical transformation and the Styling Garage house style is now one of restrained elegance. The cars in the latest model line-up bear only alloy wheels and subtle front

and rear spoilers to set them apart from the standard cars and rely on their power-operated soft-tops or gullwing doors for individuality. Perhaps this is an indication that the market has come full circle. Styling Garage does not do much mechanical work on its cars and if customers want highly tuned engines, then the power units are farmed out to AMG for preparation.

Chasing the sun on a warm summer's day has always been one of the best reasons for owning an open sports car, but the soft-top option has long since graduated to four-seater cars of all kinds, from VW Golfs to Mercedes SECs. It is no surprise, therefore, that the best-selling of all the SGS cars is the Marbella Convertible, based on the Mercedes 500SEC. Over 150 of these

Previous pages The Styling Garage Arrow's doors are based on the standard car's items, but extend into the roof to allow better access. Pop-up headlamps are integrated well and only the vents built into the rear three-quarter flanks hint at over-design. Visually, they break up a solid area

Left The detailing on the Styling Garage Arrow is superb and the stereo system is enough to rock the car on its suspension
Above The frontal aspect of the SGS car loses the Mercedes-Benz identity completely as it swoops down into an untypical wedge
Right The rear, too, could emanate from a Turin design studio

cars have left the Hamburg factory since 1981.

The Marbella has its roof and the bodywork and floorpan reinforced before the hydraulically operated, electrically controlled soft-top is fitted, and in the process, the client's car can be trimmed to any specification, some even bearing video units and cocktail bars in case the view gets boring.

While the bulk of Marbella sales were in the Arab States and the sunny south of Europe, the latest trends indicate more German customers for the car, with 19 units being sold domestically in 1985. Strangely, in a world of spiralling prices the unit cost and hence the retail price of this car is actually decreasing, as more are made and development costs are amortized: the

conversion now costs £18,600 on top of the price of a production 500SEC, which should take care of your loose change.

The Mercedes 300SL Gullwing is the undisputed classic Mercedes sports car and bearing this in mind SGS set about its own interpretation of the concept in 1982, with a gullwing version of the 500SEC. This was the car which earned it worldwide recognition and which has been the basis for many more exotic styling conversions, some of which have represented the company at international motor shows like Geneva.

The doors are based on the originals and from the side the car is indistinguishable from the standard one, apart from the door handles which are moved to a position

nearer the bottom. The roof is strengthened by a roll bar and custom-built door hangers are installed, along with the electric/hydraulic lift mechanisms. There is a manual override, just in case the battery goes flat. Apparently, the resulting structure is strong enough to withstand driving at over 100mph (161kph) with the doors open, in case you're worried about ventilation!

Of the 57 or so cars built, many left the factory with spoilers and neatly extended wheel arches covering super-wide alloy wheels and tyres, but the most radical of the gullwing cars was the Arrow, shown at Geneva in 1985. This car further disguised its Mercedes origins with a completely new front end from the bulkhead forwards that featured a

Its TV, video, writing consoles and CD/radio/cassette audio system make the Royale as close to a mobile living room as any on the road. In case of jealous neighbours any of the SGS cars can be armour-plated!

Left, far left and below The lengthened and widened Royale provides much more room than the standard Mercedes-Benz 500 saloon so that 'essential' extras like drinks cabinets and television/stereo consoles fit easily

When too much just isn't enough – Styling Garage can extend the Royale concept even further to provide face-to-face seating in the utmost luxury, with the *de rigueur* acres of wood veneer and leather for the interior

longer and more aerodynamic nose section.

In the earlier days of the bespoke motor car body, a coachbuilder might well have defined a limousine as a lengthy saloon car with four doors and a glass division separating the front and rear compartments. Usually, there would be six side windows and capacity in the rear compartment for four or five passengers to travel in comfort. The very word 'limousine' conjures up visions of uniformed chauffeurs and liveried footmen, in a world far removed from that of today's owner-driver. Yet the pampered limousine mode of travel – normally reserved for royalty, heads of state and a few privileged wealthy individuals – offers relaxed and effortless travel for the passengers while the chauffeur does the work. For the busy executive, such a car can be a mobile office, where important decisions are made, speeches written and international 'phone calls connected.

This certainly was the *raison d'être*

One of the most popular of Styling Garage designs is the Marbella, which uses the 2 + 2 Mercedes-Benz 500SEC Coupé as a base. Whereas the open-top SL Mercedes is a strict two-seater, the SGS conversion allows four passengers to travel *al fresco* in an M-B product, with a hydraulically operated roof. The Marbella is a little more restrained in its style than the Arrow Gullwing (behind), which brings the original concept, used by Mercedes-Benz in the mid-Fifties, up to date

Main picture The Marbella doesn't have to be too conservative. Little side skirts and rear valence panels can be incorporated to build the car's image, while there is no limit to what can be done to the interior

Insets Once the wood and leather have been included, what is there left to spend money on? How about specially sign-written instruments, with maybe a precious stone or two inset into the dials for good measure?

for the 600SGS-5.0 and the even longer 800SGS-5.0, both based on the 500SEL Mercedes and stretched in wheelbase 23½ inches (600mm) and 31½ inches (800mm) respectively. These cars have four to six rear seats, an electrically operated partition window and luxury appointments in noble woods, leather and velour that would do justice to the Orient Express.

But in 1985, Styling Garage decided to go one better and produce the SGS Royale, which looks more 'correct' than the other 'stretched' SGS cars. While the 600 and 800SGS cars are merely lengthened, making them seem perhaps a little ungainly, the Royale looks more proportional because it was not only stretched by 11¾ inches (300mm), but also widened by 8 inches (200mm). To even out dimensions, each of the doors was lengthened by 6 inches (150mm), so the added length and width are only really apparent inside the car or if it draws up next to a standard 500SEL.

'Elbow' room is substantially increased and there is now space for three electrically adjustable seats side-by-side. You also have plenty of room to play with the TV, video, writing consoles and CD/radio/cassette audio system, not to mention the refrigerator and cocktail bar, making this car as close to a mobile living room as any on the road. In case of threats from jealous neighbours you can order this or indeed any of the SGS cars with armour plating.

At a basic price of over £100,000 demand for the Royale is expected to be somewhat limited, but then at Styling Garage, exclusivity is a foregone conclusion.

LINER, LARGO
AND ROADSTER
TRESER

Manufacturers' parts bins are fascinating places, but is takes a very special kind of engineer to grasp the possibilities of a certain combination of bits and assemble them in a package that works well as a practical and saleable product. Two such engineers were Jorg Benzinger and Walter Treser who realized the potential of marrying the 4WD parts of the military Iltis, developed by VW, to an Audi 80 floorpan. And so the Audi Quattro was born.

The son of a hotelier, it seemed that Walter Treser was destined to enter the world of gastronomy. As a boy, however, it was technology and cars in particular that fascinated him: he was able to drive at eight, built himself a motorcycle at 14 and at 18 he proved it was possible to drive his car on two wheels. In 1962, aged 22, he passed his exams in automotive and aeronautical engineering and went to work for Daimler-Benz and then Veith Pirelli where he was put in charge of the experimental tyre department, developing low-profile tyres like the P7. Treser moved on to Audi in 1977 where he worked closely with Ferdinand Piech, head of the experimental department, and it was not long before his talent earned him the post of head of the

Preliminary Experimental Department and he became the youngest member of the Committee for Technological Strategy. With the development of the Audi Quattro under his belt, Treser undertook the organization of Audi's rally sport involvement and from March 1980 till August 1981 was head of the company's competition department.

On 1 January 1982, Treser founded his own company, Walter Treser Automobiltechnik und Design, in Ingolstadt to develop and manufacture special high-quality components for Audi cars, as well as exclusive specialized models based on Audis. On 26 August 1985, he founded the Walter Treser Automobilbau GmbH in Berlin and is currently developing his own car which is due to make its public debut at the 1987 Frankfurt Show. His

The Liner's slippery shape allows it a top speed of 180mph (290kph), making this unique Treser conversion one of the fastest estate cars in the world

company is recognized as an independent car manufacturer by the West German Federal Department of Transport.

Treser Audi is the logo you will see on the back of every Treserized Audi car, but the significance of the two names together is rather more far-reaching than is normal in motor industry relationships between a major manufacturer and a specialist tuner of that manufacturer's products. Even Alpina, unique among tuning firms in supplying completely altered cars, and which also qualifies for manufacturer's status, is unable to get partly assembled cars from BMW to do away with the need to strip cars of unwanted parts, saving the customer unnecessary expense and itself unnecessary trouble. Walter Treser, however, has this dispensation from Ingolstadt-based Audi, and since his new factory with 65 staff was opened in November 1984 just down the road from Audi, ties have never been closer.

Treser's former post as head of the Quattro rally development programme has naturally had some bearing on this, and the good relationship he has maintained with the management of Audi is a distinct advantage for him, but it would also be right to say that Audi needs Treser, too. Development work on specialist items for cars like the quattro (which officially lost its initial capital letter in 1984) can cost a big manufacturer a lot in terms of time and money so it makes good business sense to commission a small, fast-moving concern like Treser to do it. A good example of ideas adopted by Audi for its production cars would be the blacked-out tail-light assemblies used on Treserized quattros. These became standard on all factory cars from 1985 on. 'Our relationship is built on mutual respect,' says Walter Treser. 'We are not a rival to Audi, nor are we better in any way. What we offer our customers is a limited production alternative which is a freedom no large manufacturer can afford to indulge in.'

It takes experience to settle on a good balance for a modified, high-performance road car. 'We do not make competition cars here,' Treser explains. 'At the same time, our vehicles must be sufficiently improved in the customer's opinion to justify the extra outlay. It is a delicate balance.' Highly tuned cars can run into reliability problems, but where Treser engines are concerned the emphasis is on long-term durability. This is why an extra 50bhp, a mere 25 per cent increase in horsepower, is deemed appropriate for the Treser quattro.

Ever wary of fashion for its own sake, Treser's design philosophy is the traditional one of form following function, but at the same time, he only produces things that he likes himself. 'I make what I like and what I know will work in engineering terms,' he explains. 'The danger of producing everything a customer wants is that you could get unbalanced and unworkable concepts, which would not be in step with our company philosophy and may ultimately not be what the customer likes himself when he has seen it materialized.' Treser explains how the upsweep of the centre of the front spoiler on his Audi 100/200 design allows cooling air to flow around the sump and gearbox. This was something learnt on the rally programme. On the rear boot spoiler, a similar recess exists but for a different reason – so you can easily use the key on the boot lock. Following the same line of thought, the pattern of the Treser alloy wheels, while adding dynamism to the car at rest, pulls cooling air through the wheels to the brakes when on the move. What the driver of a Treser Audi will see most of, however, is the steering wheel and its design was arrived at after a long process of elimination. The final version feels right in the hands in terms of diameter, rim thickness and materials and, with its thumb cut-outs, almost forces you to hold it in the correct three and nine o'clock position

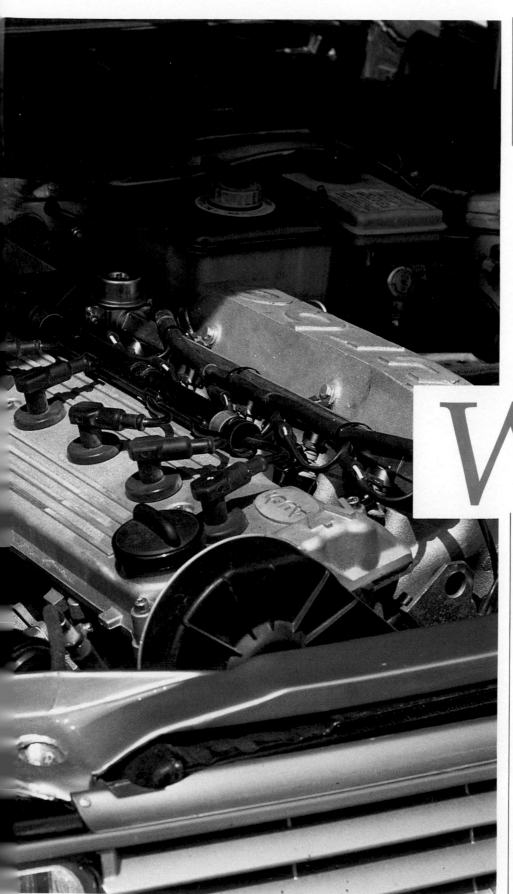

Previous pages
Although it looks like an Audi 100/200, the Treser Liner has a carefully integrated Avant back grafted on to saloon pillars to lessen the estate-car effect of the original

Left The Sport quattro engine fitted to the Liner has four valves for each of its five cylinders
Below The 'bustleback' look combines both saloon and estate lines at the rear

While there are now several examples of the Treser genius attracting envious glances around the world, one car that Walter recently made for a wealthy German client is unique. In this instance, the customer opted for the Liner bodyshell which Treser pioneered in 1983 but combined with the four-wheel-drive capability of the quattro, the versatility of the Avant and the power of the 20-valve, 300bhp quattro Sport engine.

While it would be fair to say that, due mainly to the company having a clear and consistent design policy for all its cars, quite a lot of Audi parts are interchangeable, albeit with a bit of hacking here and there, this combination had its fair share of shoehorning problems. Treser considers such cars as prototypes, and indicates that while useful lessons are learned through the building of such one-off versions, he was convinced that with the man-hours that go into solving the many technical problems – no technical problem is insurmountable in his book – he might not make any money on this car. At the end of the day the price he has to charge the customer, however rich he or she may be, has to sound realistic.

This particular customer was apparently very happy with his Treser 200 quattro but not quite satisfied with the 232bhp available from the modified 200 Turbo engine which only gave it a nominal top whack of 160mph (275kph)! Equally, just to have the required 300bhp engine in a Treserized Avant or 200 quattro was

visually inadequate for this Bavarian gentleman, so the Liner body style was pulled out of the Treser catalogue.

The Liner starts life as an Audi Avant quattro, and promptly has the last couple of feet of its roof and hatchback removed and the C-pillar and rear windscreen from the saloon grafted on. This gives the vehicle a distinctive notchback look while not detracting too much from the estate-car versatility of the Avant.

Audi is known to be experimenting with V8 engines and the quattro system has proved capable of handling up to 600bhp in suitably modified form. Handling the

300bhp of the Sport engine was therefore no tall order and the suspension required only the usual Treser springs, dampers and uprated brakes to cope. Shoehorning the new engine in was not that great a problem either and the Liner has an entire engine and transaxle transplant, including the brakes, from the Sport. The Sport engine runs a much bigger turbo unit, so underbonnet temperatures build up rather more rapidly. A small NACA duct was let into the offside leading edge of the bonnet to admit cooling air on a line that takes it over the

turbo, and a larger NACA duct sits in the centre of the bonnet. These have proved inadequate to deal with the heat soak generated by long-distance, high-speed work, however, and the latest modification provides louvres in the bonnet like those of the quattro Sport.

Although the heavy Liner is slower through the gears than the Sport, passing 60mph (97kph) in about 6.4 seconds, its more slippery shape allows it a top speed of close to 180mph (290kph), making it one of the fastest estate cars in the world.

Adding 12¼ inches (31cm) to the wheelbase and 9 ⁵⁄₁₆ inches (24cm) to the overall length of a slightly wedge-shaped saloon car is no easy task. 'The optical problems are immense', explains Walter Treser, 'if a car is not to end up looking stretched as so many of these conversions do.' The problem is particularly apparent when the lengthening is carried out to the doors, so what Treser does is to cut the roof above the trailing edge of the rear door and insert the extra section there, carefully adjusting it to

The Treser Largo is an extended version of the 100/200 Audi series, giving a refreshing variation to the many similarly converted cars from the rival Mercedes-Benz stable. The Largo's wheelbase is increased behind the rear door, and the conversion is so good that a second look is needed to confirm the extra length

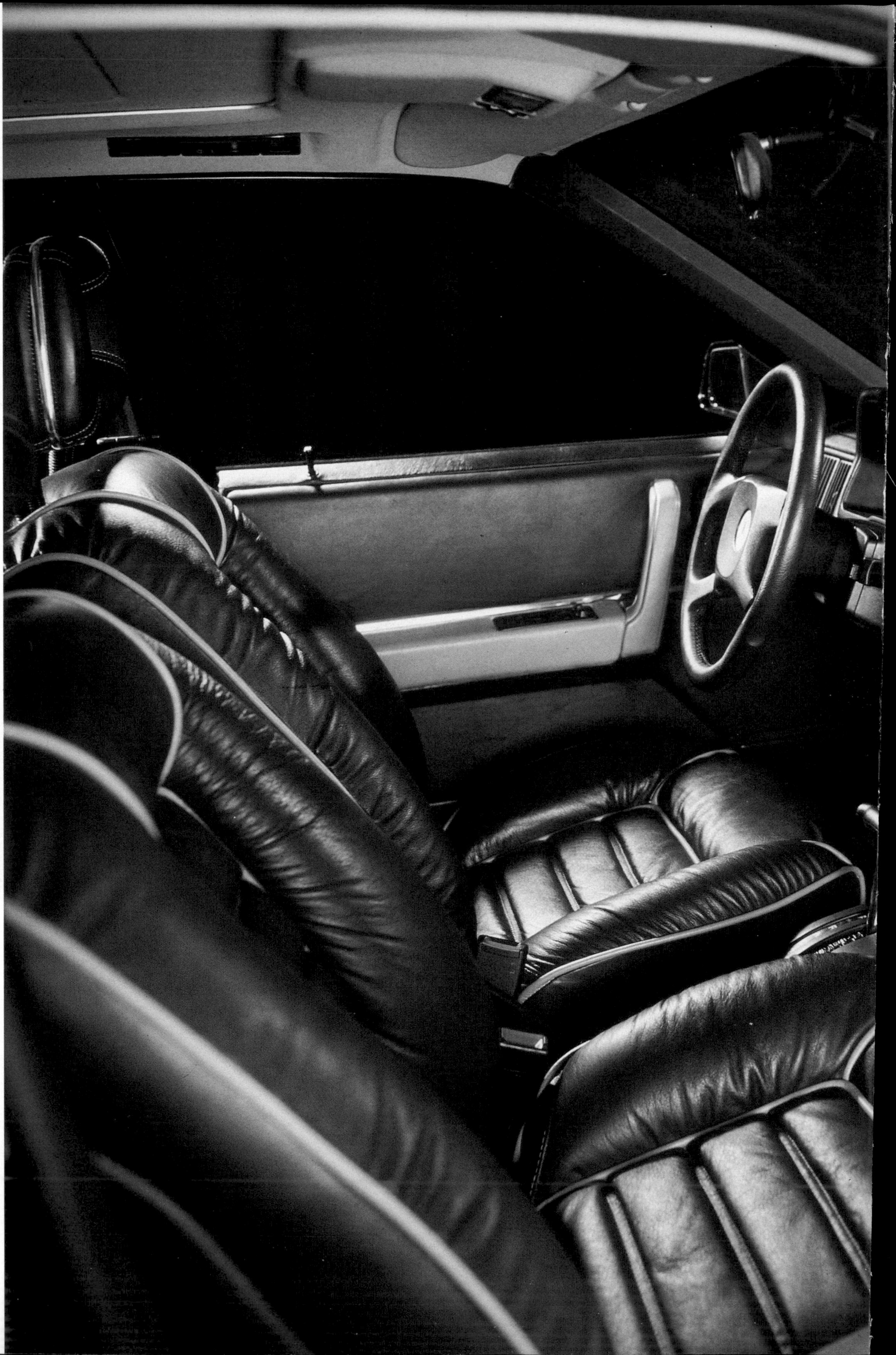

ensure that the finished product looks right. The result is a car that maintains its wedge shape consistently throughout its length and also looks symmetrical in elevation.

Inside, the increase in space in the rear is dramatic, although the standard car is already roomy. There are also special options available like TV, video, bar, telephone, stereo and so on, and of course the interior can be trimmed in leather to the owner's specification.

Left This Largo is based on the Audi 100 and has its engine boosted to 2.3 litres to provide a maximum power of 165bhp. For much more power, a four-wheel-drive chassis has to be used as a base

Far left The unabashed luxury of the Largo, with cossetting leather seats

From a sales point of view, the Largo has been a winner as an executive, high-speed limousine; for nervous VIPs an armoured, turbocharged, four-wheel-drive version is even available

The Largo can be based on any of the Audi 100/200 range, front-wheel-drive or quattro. Suspension and powerplant choice is up to the owner although, for safety reasons, Treser will not provide any power output greater than 182bhp for the front-driven cars.

From the sales point of view, the Largo has been a winner as an executive, high-speed limousine. And who knows how many VIPs have opted for the armoured, turbocharged, four-wheel-drive version also available?

I

f originality, perhaps symbolized by the '1' mark of his corporate logo (a mark which used to belong to Audi and is now his with Audi's authority), is one of Treser's trump cards, then the ace in the pack must be the quattro Roadster, the world's first four-wheel-drive, turbocharged roadster, and a most desirable car.

The idea of the roadster is not a new one for Treser. It was in fact mooted when the company was in its infancy, but Treser never does things just for their own sake, preferring careful and detailed development instead. The end result is a concept so outlandishly simple and foolproof, one is apt to wonder why it has never been done before.

A cabriolet has several

The Treser Roadster in the middle of its metamorphosis from open roadster to closed coupé. With the added advantage of open-air motoring and the power of the turbocharged engine, the Treser is without doubt one of the world's most desirable cars

disadvantages, water-proofing, noise and security being the most prominent. While a detachable hardtop is a good solution, you can't exactly take it with you, so if you are going far that can be a distinct handicap. The Treser Roadster neatly sidesteps these problems with its ingenious hinged hardtop, counterbalanced to disappear backwards and down below the rear

deck which you must first lift on its rear hinges before moving the hardtop either way. The whole operation can be completed by one person in a mere 30 seconds and does not encroach upon the standard car's boot-space. Working within the confines of the wheelbase, the design evolved from consideration of the fuel tank's position above the rear axle. Space

for the top to fold into was at a premium, hence the reduced rear seat room and the resulting length of the rear deck.

As in all open cars, the topless bodyshell of the Roadster is significantly strengthened with a welded cage of steel around the door and rear-deck areas. Of particular note is a lateral beam that runs above the floorpan between what would have been the B-pillar area and there are mandatory strengthening plates along the sills. The fit and finish of all the new body panels and glass fibre hardtop and deck are equal to the original factory parts. The leather coachbuilder's interior is also beautifully re-trimmed and a clear and complete analogue instrument panel replaces the unloved digital unit of the production car.

All this brings the weight of the Roadster to within spitting distance of that of the standard coupé quattro which would indicate that any observed performance deviation either way would be a reflection of aerodynamics rather than weight. Top speed is still 137mph (220kph) with a 0–60mph (0–97kph) time of around 7 seconds.

The first Roadster was unveiled in 1983, the conversion doubling the price of Audi's quattro to £40,000. The popularity of this car among the well-heeled has been quite staggering, with one of the first going to the Monaco royal family and another four to the Sultan of Oman who already had five Treserized quattros. An added refinement for his Roadsters, now an option for other customers, is power operation of the hood via four hydraulic rams which ensure that His Royal Highness no longer has to stop the car to alter His climate.

With the hood up, the Treser Roadster matches its coupé cousin, incorporating all the strengths of the 200bhp quattro – superb traction and stability in all weather conditions with the option of being closer to nature when the sun is shining. Its rarity value is an added bonus in a world full of Porsche 911 and Ferrari Mondial Cabriolets.

If originality is one of Treser's trump cards, then the ace in the pack must be the quattro Roadster. Its rarity value is an added bonus in a world full of Porsche 911 and Ferrari Mondial Cabriolets

Left The digital instrumentation of the standard quattro has been replaced with functional race-car-like dials on the Roadster

Top The Treser Roadster ahead of a Treser-modified quattro
Above Even a Treser pilot needs an excess of decibels....

JAGUAR XJS 6.0 LITRE
TWR

Too many conversions create an imbalance in the final work, amplifying some of the strengths of the basic car, perhaps to the detriment of some of its other qualities. You will find no such shortcomings when you drive the TWR Jaguar XJS 6.0 litre, for Tom Walkinshaw and his team have taken the smooth, cultured and beautifully engineered V12 coupé and refined it still further.

Tom Walkinshaw's design on the Jaguar XJS Coupé is very much an understatement, but the integral front bumper/spoiler makes the 'Big Cat' that much more attractive

When you look at Jaguar's traditional racing heritage, you realize that this is a car the factory itself quite rightfully should have been expected to produce. It is a stunning yet elegant looker, which produces 380bhp from an engine enlarged from 5.3 to 6.0 litres. The firmer suspension set-up takes the heavy car round corners as if on rails and yet hardly mars the silent and graceful ride over less than perfect surfaces. A steering-valve modification adds real weight and precision to the helm. And when you understand that many of the mechanical improvements on the standard road cars were developed in the heat of the European Touring Car (ETC) Championship, it brings home the truth of the old adage that racing does truly improve the breed. In this, Tom Walkinshaw Racing (TWR) has been more successful than most. With a strong basic product to develop, TWR conceived a winning formula which brought the big Jaguars five outright successes in the ETC Championship in 1983 and Tom the title of Champion the following year. The crowning victory for the TWR Jaguars was winning the 1985 James Hardie 1000 at Australia's demanding, mountainous Bathurst Circuit where the cars qualified 1-2-3 and finished first and third.

But why Jaguar, particularly when TWR had a long association with BMW and Mazda? Tom Walkinshaw does not do things by half measures, and to win the ETC Championship outright, he had to have the best-

handling and most powerful car. With its double-wishbone suspension and 5.3-litre V12 engine, the heavy Jaguar had the basic ingredients of a potential winner. And so in 1982, entirely on TWR's own initiative, Tom proved to the world that his XJS could compete against the factory works BMWs. Fortunately for his enterprise, Jaguar's new boss at the time, John Egan, fully recognized the value, in terms of corporate image and worldwide sales, of his cars winning races and so the following year TWR found itself with a healthy racing budget from the factory as well as a basic product improved in line with the attitude of the new management at Coventry.

Having proven the quality and durability of his racing parts, Tom Walkinshaw set about the task of preparing a package to improve road-going Jaguars for enthusiast owners.

First in line for attention was the bodywork of the classic but ageing coupé. The TWR body-styling package was designed by Peter Stevens, now head of design at Lotus Cars, and uses RRIM for the front bumper/spoiler section, giving resilience to paint chipping by flying stones, and glass fibre for the rear and side sills. A neat rear spoiler adds the finishing touch to the bodywork. This allows the powered radio aerial to work through a hole in the moulding, though you have to remember to switch off the radio when you want to open the boot!

The simple but elegant 8 × 16 – . inch (20 × 41cm) alloy wheels are made for TWR by Speedline in Italy and wear 225/50VR16 and 245/55VR16 Goodyear NCT tyres front

The TWR team has taken the smooth, cultured and beautifully engineered V12 coupé and refined it to produce this stunning yet elegant looker – this is indeed the ultimate Jaguar

and rear respectively. The size differential is for reasons of gearing, ride and grip. Part of the brief was to lower the car slightly and uprate the over-soft suspension while improving the breakaway characteristics, particularly in the wet. Firmer bushes help control all round and new rear radius arms prevent the wheels toeing out when your right foot removes the 380bhp in haste. The rear springs are left alone but the front ones are uprated, or made stronger, by 8 per cent. Gas-filled Bilstein dampers are used all round, which are not far from the standard settings on bump but are much firmer on the rebound.

The ability to stop should never be in question when a car is capable of 170mph (274kph). Four-pot racing-style calipers clamp ventilated discs at the front while two-pot units work on larger-than-standard vented discs at the rear, replacing the solid discs. Interestingly, these new calipers and pads weigh only 8lb (3.6kg) each compared with the 21lb (9.5kg) of the standard items. Chassis work is completed by a modified steering rack and new valves in the Adwest power steering which increase feel by 20 per cent.

The mechanical highlight of a standard XJS is its 300bhp 5.3-litre V12 engine which can gain about 7 per cent in power with a less restrictive exhaust system. While the TWR XJS gains some performance from having a drag coefficient some

Above left The detailing on the TWR Jaguar is excellent and much trouble has been taken to improve the look of the original product without either adding too much of a new and separate identity or detracting more from the often-criticized original

Below left The aerodynamics of the TWR Jaguar are bound to be efficient, as Tom Walkinshaw has learned much about the Jaguar XJS by many successful forays into saloon-car racing. More often than not, his Jaguars have been the first past the chequered flag in the races they have entered

12.7 per cent better than standard, with front and rear lift reduced by a staggering 60 and 88 per cent respectively, fairly minor engine modifications would still not have given the car a decisive edge over opposition such as the Porsche 928S. There is no substitute for cubic capacity and so the TWR engineers went for 6.0 litres achieved by a long-throw crankshaft. Other internal alterations include special forged multiple-taper pistons and modified cylinder heads. The engine has also been stripped down and then rebuilt to a complete specification to produce optimum performance – a complete engine blueprint. Simply using a higher compression ratio and high-lift camshafts would have given the desired power increase, but TWR recognizes that the Jaguar is a smooth, swift, long-distance machine, not a lumpy, high-revving sprinter, so it has avoided taking the route that would have detracted from driveability. This alternative has allowed a gain in power to 380bhp which is put into perspective by the fact that the 5.3-litre ETC racing XJS puts out about 450bhp. With a massive torque of 385lb ft, 0–60mph (0–97kph) is achieved in 5.6 seconds and top speed is 170mph (274kph), compared with the standard car's

The only give-away points in the TWR XJS which distinguish it from the standard item are the grippy leather steering wheel and the gear lever which dips into a ZF manual gearbox to further increase the car's performance. The standard car has a power-sapping automatic gearbox

of 6.5 seconds and 153mph (246kph).

Some of this improvement is due to the much better use of available power made by the ZF five-speed manual gearbox that TWR uses in place of the three-speed automatic. This box was developed for the V12-powered BMW that never materialized and Tom put down the money for 40 of these, which retail at a price of £6,700 each.

Much of the appeal of an XJS has to do with the distinct and individual character of the car – the view down the long bonnet, the snug cabin full of the smell and sight of Connolly hide, distinguished-looking elm burr and the highly polished chrome fittings. Not much has been changed there, except for installing matching

Scottish tweed inserts in the seats to stop you sliding around under the lateral forces that this modified car so easily generates. A four-spoke, leather-bound steering wheel has also been added, and works beautifully with the new steering rack and valving to help you plot your course around lesser machinery.

In a short span of time, TWR has appointed eight agents in the UK, as well as in the USA, Australia, Germany and Japan, so perhaps the only limit to the number of these cars on the road is the number of Jaguar owners (Tom Walkinshaw can produce body kits and engines for the XJ saloons as well as sports versions) who are prepared to dig deep into their wallets to find the £50,000 that buys a fully specified TWR XJS. That may be double the amount Jaguar charges for a standard car but Tom Walkinshaw leaves nobody in doubt that his is the ultimate Jaguar.

The rear wing takes the eye away from the 'flying buttresses' of the XJS design to give the car a more purposeful air. The car has speed to match its looks

W2
VECTOR

Previous pages The Vector is not just a styling design, but is a whole sports car concept and one which is as modern as this minute. It takes the idea of flying on the ground one stage further, and its sleek and low look would not be out of place on a race track

Below and inset left Dynamic from every angle, the Vector is more about image than practicality

Inset right The Chevrolet Camaro-based classic 5.7-litre V8 can produce upwards of 500bhp normally, but has 600bhp, courtesy of twin!turbochargers

Like aircraft, most truly exotic cars, apart from Porsches, require a lot of 'down time' for maintenance if they are to be kept at the absolute peak of performance and reliability.

Thus, while the looks, technical execution and most certainly the performance of the Vector W2 make it almost a 'tactical aircraft for street use', it was designed to be user-friendly from the servicing and

maintenance point of view to enable its wealthy owners to get as much posing time as possible out of their £100,000 cars.

It was the urge to build the world's most exotic and yet convenient-to-own sports car that started company owner Gerry Wiegert on the road to building the Vector. The seed of the idea grew around modular construction and good availability of parts. The bodywork is a composite of Kevlar and graphite with a Formula One-style semi-monocoque chassis. But here the Vector deviates from the norm with a chassis construction more akin to a military jet aircraft than a racing car. The aluminium box-section side members are joined to the honeycomb floor by aerospace epoxy and high-stress rivets and the chassis comes out weighing only 350lb (158kg). As the car was tested for three years on roads and racing circuits in the USA, Europe and the Middle East, durability in everyday use should never be a problem.

The front suspension is classic racing car, with unequal-length double wishbones, adjustable Koni dampers and an anti-roll bar. To make sure the rear wheels stay upright under all conditions, Wiegart uses a de Dion axle which, although bulkier in terms of space utilization,

works perfectly in a mid-engined design where space is not a priority. Steering is by rack and pinion with 3.2 turns lock-to-lock.

When a car is capable of over 200mph (322kph) and can pass 60mph (97kph) in under 4 seconds from rest, its stopping arrangements have to be something out of the ordinary. Consequently, the Vector uses AP-Lockhead, 12-inch (30.5cm) diameter, ventilated discs all round with a hydraulically assisted sensor to regulate pedal pressure and stop the driver too easily locking up the wheels. If the Vector was being designed today, it would probably wear ABS anti-lock brakes, but that technology had not been perfected in 1980. The massive rubberwear on the car is 50 series Pirelli P7s and these are mounted on 9 × 15-inch (23 × 38cm) and 12 × 15-inch (31 × 38cm) alloy wheels.

Lack of funds prevented Wiegart

from designing a new engine, so he opted for the 5.7-litre Chevrolet V8 which he regards as the most effective racing engine ever built. The Vector engines are carefully stripped, balanced and strengthened internally. New pistons of lower compression are installed to cope with the forced aspiration from two Garrett AiResearch H3 turbochargers which blow through a Bosch K-Jetronic CIS fuel injection system suitably upgraded with high-flow injectors. The resulting engines – in street legal form – develop 600bhp at 6,500rpm and 620lb ft of torque at 4,200rpm. Should the driver feel threatened at the traffic lights, although the odds of meeting a Koenig twin-turbo Ferrari are fairly slim, it is possible to adjust the blow-off pressure of the twin Boost-Guard wastegates from inside the car to allow an even greater output for a short time!

The looks, technical execution and most certainly the performance of the Vector W2 make it almost a tactical aircraft for street use

The styling of the Vector is dramatic, to say the least. The body is smooth and angular with no protruding door mirrors or trim to interrupt the flowing, red lines. The front half of the nose section and the rear panel are moulded in urethane which deforms on impact and then slowly returns to its original shape. The nose-cone incorporates a pair of driving lights, also used for flashing slower cars, and a pair of NACA ducts beside the main intake help to draw in air for the radiator, oil-cooler and inter-coolers. Perhaps the least well-executed detail on the front is the mesh of the front spoiler ducts for the brake-cooling. The doors lift vertically on front hinges and oleo-pneumatic struts and the side windows and front screen are dark-tinted glass. The highlight of the rear of the car is the optional rear wing which costs around £3,500 and is of adjustable aerofoil section.

Wiegert found designing the Vector for easy maintenance so simple. It is possible to remove the engine without the transmission or the rest of the drivetrain, for instance, which saves labour time.

If the inside of the Vector reminds you of the cockpit of a tandem, two-seater aircraft, that is hardly surprising as bar graph instruments, electrical switches and seat harnesses are straight out of an F-15 Eagle jet fighter. Electrically adjustable Recaro seats are standard equipment but if it is absolutely necessary to carry an extra passenger then a bench-type front seat is on the options list. This arrangement is made possible by the complete absence of a transmission tunnel in the uncluttered interior.

The Vector carries 24 Blaupunkt speakers in the doors and door jambs, linked to a top-of-the range Berlin radio/cassette unit with remote control and to the CB set mandatory in the US for early warning of

'Smokeys'. Whether the standard-issue police car could catch up with a Vector, however, is far from certain! The high-tech look is completed by a calculator keyboard-type ignition system with its own code.

Vehicle Design Force, the company established to manufacture the Vector, started off making 25 cars per year and it was no surprise that the Saudi Arabian royal family ordered the first few cars off the line. VDF requires a five-figure deposit and a letter of credit from the customer's bank when an order for this hand-crafted supercar is placed.

The Vector W2 provides a formidable challenge to the Italian and German supercar manufacturers who have dominated the market for so long, and at last places the USA well and truly on the map as an exotic car maker.

The Vector W2 doesn't look quite as well proportioned from the back (below), but it looks every inch a true classic from the front.

The lift-up doors (above) are similar to those used on the Lamborghini Countach, its much slower rival!

MAGNUM

VESTATEC

The Vestatec Magnum has two great strengths – disguise and surprise. If anyone succeeded in guessing that under the swoopy exterior lies a 3-Series BMW, then the 3.5-litre straight-six engine would add yet another dimension to the puzzle.

The Magnum was dreamed up by Vestatec, a firm which markets body styling parts and packages throughout Europe and supplies highly original equipment parts to several major manufacturers, and gave Vestatec a chance to develop a unique, albeit expensive showcase for their talents.

Initial work on the car was mechanical and was sub-contracted to Hartge, the famous German BMW tuner. Its first task was to transplant the big block six-cylinder engine from a BMW 735i saloon into the confined 3-Series engine bay. Not content with the 218bhp offered by the Munich firm, Hartge engineers proceeded to modify the cylinder-head and add a high-lift camshaft and a free-flow exhaust manifold to raise output to a healthy 250bhp at 6,200rpm, torque being in the region of 251lb ft at 4,000rpm. This is a fairly mild state of tune for such an engine and you can have closer to 300bhp on demand, but if you have an insatiable lust for tractable horsepower, then the only answer is the 24-valve twin-camshaft M-Power unit as fitted to the BMW M1, M5 and M635CSi. This develops a lusty 286bhp which Hartge claims it can further increase to 330bhp without spoiling driveability!

Apart from the front suspension which was donated by a 5-Series BMW, the other major mechanical components are taken from the 635CSi and include the close-ratio Getrag gearbox, heavy-duty clutch, limited-slip differential, rear suspension and ABS anti-lock braking system. The springs and dampers are re-rated to compensate for the difference in weight between the Magnum and the 635CSi, and with the limited-slip differential and 205/50VR15 tyres on Vestatec-designed alloy wheels, all this chassis development creates a level of handling in the region of manageable.

Before returning the car to Vestatec, Hartge added an auxiliary 7.7 gallon (35-litre) fuel tank to supplement the existing 12 gallon (55-litre) capacity. This was an indication not just of the extra thirst of the bigger engine, but also of the manner in which the car was expected to be driven.

With the mechanical alterations thus completed, it was left to Vestatec to perform the visual magic. Its first task involved removing the entire front of the car from the bulkhead forward and remodelling it in glass fibre. The designers were after a more aerodynamic, sloping nose which first meant extending the front to clear the engine and sub-frame before angling it down towards the new bumper/spoiler section. Pop-up headlamps were part of the design brief and these are off-the-shelf Porsche 944 units. The bonnet itself is a new glass fibre part with a vented power bulge and extends backwards to conceal the single windscreen wiper.

Proportionately, the bluff front of the 3-Series BMW has as large an air intake area as any production car today so it comes as no surprise to learn that the Magnum ran into overheating problems in early testing. The large number of vents on the front of the car now provide adequate cooling and these have been adopted as a theme and used along the side panels in front of the rear wheels and on the rear air dam. The waistline extension is also formed from glass fibre, as is the window louvre, while the rear spoiler is of soft deformable polyurethane, a visual illusion to lead the onlooker into believing that the Magnum is a hatchback and so disguise its origins. The deception is further enhanced by the coachbuilders removing a section of the roof above the C-pillar which has been raked to a more acute angle.

The final work was on the interior, for which the car was dispatched to Gemballa who re-upholstered it,

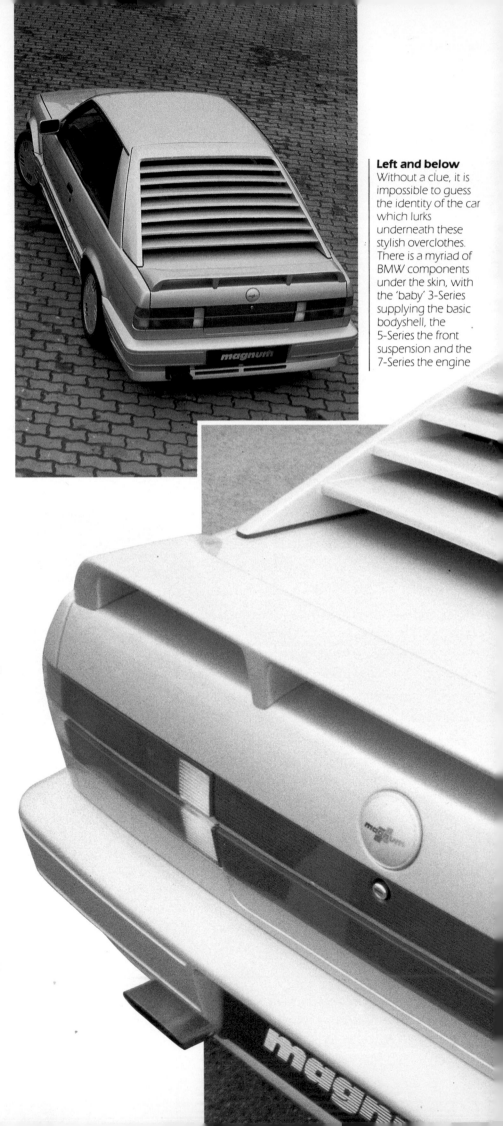

Left and below
Without a clue, it is impossible to guess the identity of the car which lurks underneath these stylish overclothes. There is a myriad of BMW components under the skin, with the 'baby' 3-Series supplying the basic bodyshell, the 5-Series the front suspension and the 7-Series the engine

The finished car underwent rigorous testing procedures, passing with flying colours, and power on tap is ferocious

including the electrically operated Recaro seats, in soft leather. Additional instruments were mounted on top of the dash and include a voltmeter, oil temperature gauge and oil pressure gauge, and the final touches were a four-spoke steering wheel with Magnum boss and a 300-watt sound system.

Before the finished car could be offered for sale, it had to undergo the rigorous German TUV testing procedure which ensures that no sub-standard or unsafe product reaches the consumer. The Magnum passed with flying colours and during speed trials, the TUV authorities established a top speed of 160mph (257kph). A similar-engined Hartge 335i with spoilers manages

Inset and right
There is more than a hint of Porsche 924 to the front of the Magnum which further complicates the identification job
Far right Power is provided by a tuned 3.5-litre engine which pushes the little car to a top speed of 160mph (258kph) and enables it to accelerate to 60mph (97kph) in 6.2secs

only 154mph (248kph) which proves the aerodynamic efficiency of the Magnum. At lower speeds, there is nothing in it and both cars accelerate from 0–60mph (0–97kph) in 6.2 seconds.

Such power in a relatively short wheelbase means that the 'ordinary' Magnum, not to mention the 330bhp version, is quite a handful. Power on instant tap is ferocious, to say the least, and if called upon abruptly or at the wrong moment can be rather dramatic. Vestatec appreciates that such a level of performance may not be every customer's cup of tea, so they offer just the visual package for £7,700. The Gemballa interior with the 300 watt hi-fi is a snip at £3,250 and the whole shooting match, with the 3.5-litre power plant, costs a whopping £38,500.

The company will need to sell a few Magnums to recoup the £90,000 invested in development work, but when a product is of this level of quality and individuality, that can only be a matter of time.

ZIMMER

A sure-fire method of making money in the American specialist car business is to combine the appearance of a Thirties car with the convenience and mechanical specification of a modern, mass-produced vehicle. The 'right mix' in the recent past has been obtained by stripping the body off, say, a Ford

RR

RR

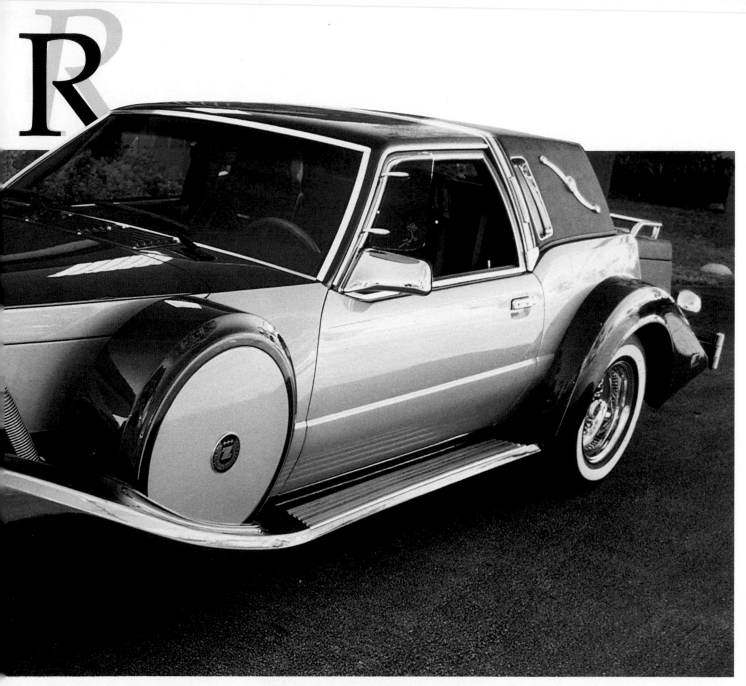

LTD model, and mounting on its chassis frame a two- or four-seater open body, styled with flowing wings, outside-mounted spare wheels, exposed headlights, outside flexible exhaust pipes and most important of all, a sculptured chromium-plated radiator shell, surmounted by a mascot of some description.

It is the look that sells this type of vehicle, especially to American buyers who lust after the image of what they see as a 'classic car', but refuse to forego the convenience of modern automotive technology. They want air-conditioning, power-assisted steering and brakes and cruise control, plus the benefits of being able to get their car serviced at any corner service shop, with every spare part on the shelf. It is for these reasons that the ersatz classic, or as the maker of the Zimmer puts it, the 'neo-classic', has come into fashion, with many manufacturers attempting to deliver what the customer wants and stay in business.

Many of these neo-classics have been automotive disasters, hurriedly (and badly) designed, with scrappy, inconsistent build quality, clumsy styling and awkward proportions. They enjoyed a brief heyday before this notoriously fickle market found them out and stopped buying them. The fading-away of some companies engaged in this field was accelerated by their real lack of any strong financial backing, plus a poor cash flow.

There is, however, a car available today in the USA that has more than enough financial backing to support it through its early years, and to sustain it until it generates the level of income that all specialist makers dream of. That car is the Zimmer.

The Zimmer is built in Pompano Beach, Florida, and since its earliest days has displayed enough stamina to stay the course. The Zimmer Corporation uses a Ford Mustang model for the base, removing the front and rear body sections, which are then replaced with stylized components, giving the car the

'classic' look. The presence of the McPherson-type front suspension is very cleverly disguised. The upper mounts for this type of suspension need to be located higher than either the twin-wishbone independent, or solid axle, style of springing. So Zimmer skillfully utilizes the headlight pods and the inside front wing area to contain the McPherson turrets without introducing a bulge in the wings or bonnet.

The car has all the 'image' attractions demanded of it by the buying public: inside there are seats by Recaro, electrically adjustable and covered in real leather; the leather is treated to look and smell like vinyl, however, because the customer is more used to vinyl than real leather! There is also a burled-walnut instrument panel containing a full set of visible dials, a splendid Nardi, leather-rimmed, 24-carat gold-plated, framed steering wheel and luxurious carpets. In the rear of the passenger compartment is a German crystal flower vase, right next to the opera window. On the outside are

Previous pages Nothing suits the American taste more than the style of a vintage car with modern practicality

Left and inset The Zimmer's interior boasts plenty of wood trimming, but not the vintage aura of the exterior

The car has all the 'image' attractions demanded of it by the buying public — an extravaganza of luxurious additions and finishing touches

items such as glass wind deflectors, with floral etchings, mounted on either side of the windscreen frame, a luggage trunk with twin leather belts, and as an option, a teak- and chromium-framed luggage rack to go on top. The rear three-quarter body panels carry fake frame tensioners, just like the real things on vintage Aston Martin or Mercedes-Benz convertibles. Twin wind horns grace the front-of-radiator area, side flexible exhaust pipes sweep out of each side of the bonnet to enter the tops of the front wings, and to finish off this extravaganza the radiator is crowned by an eagle seemingly plunging down on its prey.

The bodywork additions are made in high-quality, heavy-weight glass fibre with a sprayed finish, but the surface quality of these panels does not really match the Ford centre section, displaying a less than flat finish by comparison. But the finished Zimmer certainly has presence; it

Above All the trappings of excess: the embellishments which abound on the Zimmer are for its image rather than its dynamic performance. In a country where conformity in automobile design has been the norm and where mass-production deviation has resulted in bankruptcy, the Zimmer allows hand-made individuality

Left and below
The Thirties ornate
styling is not allowed
to interfere with the
car's purpose. It still
has to be an
adequate performer
with Eighties
refinement and
high-tech luxury

looks the part, and consequently has
enjoyed large sales. There are three
models to choose from, all with two
doors: the Golden Spirit Coupé,
which sells for about £42,000, the
Formal, up another £5,100, and the
Convertible at some £51,000.

Leaving the on-the-road
performance of the Zimmer aside,
there is really only one criticism that
can be levelled at the car's
appearance: the road wheel
diameter is approximately 2-3 inches
(5-8cm) too small. The wire wheels
are of very good quality, but being
that bit too small, they rather detract

from the 'classic' look of the Zimmer. For the purists (who probably would not be interested in the Zimmer anyway), the outside exhausts are rather odd, as they exit the bonnet side panels some 4 inches (10cm) in front of the actual engine manifold, and after entering the tops of the wings they go no further! Of course, they operate purely as a styling gimmick, and as such are very effective, but can be rather disappointing once the deception is discovered. Some will also cast a jaundiced eye over the turn signals

mounted on the tops of the front wings, which come from the lowly VW Beetle, but work very well with the overall image of the car, as they are of Germanic quality and meet the US Department of Transport regulations, adding a little normality to the slightly outrageous, 'over-the-top' appearance of the Zimmer.

A prospective buyer of a Zimmer Convertible, the top price model, was once spotted walking around the car several times without saying a word. She finally halted at the front, eyes glistening, and said, 'Oh, it's absolutely BEAUTIFUL! I love it, and I

don't care how much it costs.' The woman concerned could obviously see herself zipping along Sunset Drive on a Saturday evening, drawing admiring glances from everyone, and as far as she was concerned that's what it's all about!

The Zimmer has more than an air of Excalibur about it, but underneath the Ford Mustang base provides a known quantity in handling and performance

G L O S S A R Y

A-pillar   The front structure rising from the car's waistline to the roof

ABS   Anti-lock braking system. A system where either an electrical or mechanical device prevents the wheels locking and thus losing their retardation efficiency

Analogue form   Dial instrumentation, rather than digital read-out

B-pillar   The central structure rising from the car's waistline to the roof

Bhp   Brake horse-power. A commonly used measure of engine work rate

Blueprint   The process whereby an engine is re-manufactured to exact tolerances in its specification, thereby liberating more power. Production engines are some way from optimum

Cd   Coefficient of drag. A measurement of a car's aerodynamic efficiency. The smaller the number, the less drag there is to slow the car down

CdA   The Cd multiplied by the car's frontal area to give an overall air-penetration figure

C-pillar   The rear structure rising from the car's waistline to the roof

DCOE   A type of Weber carburettor, widely used in German and Italian engines

DOHC   Double overhead camshafts. A form of valve gear in the engine

FIA   Fédération Internationale de l'Automobile. The international ruling body of motor sport

4WD   Four-wheel drive

G force   Gravitational force. A measure of a car's overall cornering capability can be obtained by measuring the lateral g force

Group C cars   A class of sports car competing in the World Sports Car Championship. Group A are road-going sports cars; group B are racing sports cars developed from road-going sports cars; and group C are sports cars specially developed for racing

GRP   Glass-reinforced plastic, commonly known as glass fibre

Homologation A system whereby the motor sport's ruling body lists certain cars or parts eligible for use in competition

HUD   Head-up display. A system whereby the car instrumentation is reflected in the windscreen to enable the driver to keep his head up whilst driving

IMSA GTP   International Motor Sports Association Grand Touring Prototype. A class of American sports-car racing

Indy races   The premier class of single-seater motor racing in the USA, originating at the Indianapolis circuit

Kevlar   A very strong composite plastic

Lb ft   A unit of measurement applied to torque, or twisting force

LCD   Liquid-crystal display, as used in car instrumentation

LED   Light-emitting diodes, as used in car instrumentation

NACA ducts   Air-intake vents sculptured into a car's body

Opera window   A small window, usually oval, set into a car's C pillars (see above)

Pace car   A vehicle which leads Indy-type race cars (see above) on their parade lap and which is used to head the field at a reduced pace when there is a track obstruction

Psi   Pounds per square inch. A measure of pressure

PU-RIM   Polyurethane injection moulding, a way of making plastics

Q-car   A term used to describe a modified car which looks standard. It stems from the First World War when submarine-hunters were disguised to look like fishing boats — they were called Q-boats

RRIM   Reinforced reaction injection moulding

SFI   Sequential fuel injection

Targa   A roof design first used by Porsche in which the solid roof panel can be lifted off and stowed in the car

T-top   A variation on the targa theme (see above), but with two distinct roof panels separated by a fore-to-aft bracing 'T' strut

TUV   Technischer Uberwachungsverein. A German agency empowered to issue type-approval

INDEX

ACKNOWLEDGMENTS

The publishers would like to thank the following organizations and individuals for their kind permission to reproduce the photographs in this book:

Buick 54-5, 56, 57, 58, 59

Laurie Caddell/Orbis 120-1, 122, 123, 124, 125, 126-7

Brian Chittock 136-7, 138, 139, 142-3

Custom Car 224-5, 226, 227, 228, 229

Dodge 60-1, 62, 63, 64-5

CW Editorial 44-5

Ian Kuah 46, 47, 48, 49, 50-1, 52, 53, 98-9, 100, 101, 102-3, 104-5, 106-7, 108-9, 110, 111, 112-13, 176-7, 178-9, 180, 181, 182-3, 194-5, 196-7, 198, 199, 200-1, 202, 203, 206, 207 bottom, 208-9, 210, 211, 212-13, 214-15

Hans G. Lehmann 92-3, 148, 149, 184-5, 186, 187, 188-9 bottom, 190-1, 192-3, 204-5, 207 top

John McGovren 70, 71, 80-1, 82, 83, 84, 85

Mazda 114-15, 116, 117, 118, 119

Motorpresse 72-3, 76 top and bottom, 78-9

Richard Newton 12-13, 14, 15, 16, 17

Rinspeed 150-1

Saab 152-3, 154-5, 156-7, 158, 159

Rainer Schlegelmilch 40-1, 42, 43, 74, 75, 76-7, 88-9, 140, 141

Peter Vann 6-7, 8-9, 10-11, 18-19, 20-1, 22, 23, 24-5, 26-7, 28-9, 30, 31, 32-3, 34-5, 36, 37, 38-9, 86-7, 90, 91, 93, 94-5, 96, 97, 128-9, 130, 131, 132, 133, 134-5, 144-5, 146, 147, 160-1, 162, 163, 164, 165, 166, 167, 168-9, 170, 171, 172, 173, 174-5, 188, 189 top, 194 inset, 195 inset, 216-7, 218, 219, 220, 221, 222, 223

Bill Warner/Orbis 230-1, 232, 233, 234, 235, 236-7

Nick Wright 66-7, 68, 69

The author and publishers would also like to thank the following companies and individuals for their help: Clarion (UK) Ltd; Koenig Specials GmbH; the staff of Panther Cars; the press departments of Aston Martin, Austin Rover, Buick, Dodge, Mazda Cars (UK) Ltd, Porsche Cars (GB) Ltd and Saab; Vittorio Strosek and family; Thomson & Taylor (Brooklands) Ltd, UK agents for Brabus, Styling Garage and Treser; and Tom Walkinshaw Racing.

The pieces on the Hooper Bentley Turbo R (pages 80-5), the Excalibur (pages 66-71) and the Zimmer (pages 230-5) are by John McGovren, and the Buick Wildcat (pages 54-9) and the Dodge M4S (pages 60-5) are by Greg Emmerson.

240